Student Handbook to Psychology

Social Psychology

Volume VII

Student Handbook to Psychology

Social Psychology

Volume VII

JEFFREY D. HOLMES

SHEILA K. SINGH

Bernard C. Beins
General Editor

Facts On File
An Infobase Learning Company

Student Handbook to Psychology: Social Psychology
Copyright © 2012 Jeffrey D. Holmes and Sheila K. Singh

> Facts On File, Inc.
> An Imprint of Infobase Learning
> 132 West 31st Street
> New York NY 10001

Library of Congress Cataloging-in-Publication Data
Student handbook to psychology / [edited by] Bernard C. Beins.
   v. ; cm.
  Includes bibliographical references and index.
  Contents: v. 1. History, perspectives, and applications / Kenneth D. Keith—v. 2. Methods and measurements / Bernard C. Beins—v. 3. Brain and mind / Michael Kerchner—v. 4. Learning and thinking / Christopher M. Hakala and Bernard C. Beins—v. 5. Developmental psychology / Lynn Shelley—v. 6. Personality and abnormal psychology / Janet F. Carlson—v. 7. Social psychology / Jeffrey D. Holmes and Sheila K. Singh.
  ISBN 978-0-8160-8280-3 (set : alk. paper)—ISBN 978-0-8160-8281-0 (v. 1 : alk. paper)—ISBN 978-0-8160-8286-5 (v. 2 : alk. paper)—ISBN 978-0-8160-8285-8 (v. 3 : alk. paper)—ISBN 978-0-8160-8284-1 (v. 4 : alk. paper)—ISBN 978-0-8160-8282-7 (v. 5 : alk. paper)—ISBN 978-0-8160-8287-2 (v. 6 : alk. paper)—ISBN 978-0-8160-8283-4 (v. 7 : alk. paper) 1. Psychology—Textbooks. I. Beins, Bernard.
  BF121.S884 2012
  150—dc23   2011045277

Text design by Erika K. Arroyo
Cover design by Takeshi Takahashi
Composition by EJB Publishing Services
Cover printed by Yurchak Printing, Landisville, Pa.
Book printed and bound by Yurchak Printing, Landisville, Pa.
Date printed: September 2012
Printed in the United States of America

This book is printed on acid-free paper.

CONTENTS

PREFACE

Behavior is endlessly fascinating. People and other animals are complicated creatures that show extraordinary patterns of abilities, intelligence, social interaction, and creativity along with, unfortunately, problematic behaviors. All of these characteristics emerge because of the way the brain interprets incoming information and directs our responses to that information.

This seven-volume **Student Handbook to Psychology** set highlights important and interesting facets of thought and behavior. It provides a solid foundation for learning about psychological processes associated with growth and development, social issues, thinking and problem solving, and abnormal thought and behavior. Most of the major schools and theories related to psychology appear in the books in the series, albeit in abbreviated form. Because psychology is such a highly complex and diverse discipline, these volumes present a broad overview of the subject rather than a complete and definitive treatise. Such a work, in fact, would be difficult (if not impossible) because psychological scientists are still searching for answers to a great number of questions. If you are interested in delving in more depth into specific areas of psychology, we have provided a bibliography of accessible readings to help you fill in the details.

The volumes in this series follow the order that you might see in a standard presentation on a variety of topics, but each book stands alone and the series does not need to be read in any particular order. In fact, you can peruse individual chapters in each volume at will, seeking out and focusing on those topics that interest you most. On the other hand, if you do choose to read through a complete volume, you will find a flow of information that connects related sections of the books, providing a coherent overview of the entire discipline of psychology.

The authors of the seven volumes in this series are experts in their respective fields, so you will find psychological concepts that are up to date and that reflect the most recent advances in scientific knowledge about thought and behavior. In addition, each of the authors is an excellent writer who has presented the information in an interesting and compelling fashion. Although some of the material and many of the ideas are complex, the authors have done an outstanding job of conveying those ideas in ways that are both interesting and effective.

In *History, Perspectives, and Applications*, Professor Kenneth Keith of the University of San Diego has woven historical details into a tapestry that shows how psychological questions originated within a philosophical framework, incorporated biological concepts, and ultimately evolved into a single scientific discipline that remains interconnected with many other academic and scientific disciplines. Dr. Keith has identified the major figures associated with the development of the field of psychology as well as the social forces that helped shape their ideas.

In *Methods and Measurements*, I illustrate how psychologists create new knowledge through research. The volume presents the major approaches to research and explains how psychologists develop approaches to research that help us answer questions about complex aspects of behavior. Without these well-structured and proven research methods, we would not have much of the information we now have about behavior. Furthermore, these methods, approaches, and practices provide confidence that the knowledge we do have is good knowledge, grounded in solid research.

Many people are under the impression that each thought or behavior is a single thing. In *Brain and Mind*, Professor Michael Kerchner of Washington College dispels this impression by showing how the myriad structures and functions of our brain work in unison to create those seemingly simple and one-dimensional behaviors. As the author explains, each behavior is really the result of many different parts of the brain engaging in effective communication with one another. Professor Kerchner also explains what occurs when this integration breaks down.

Learning and Thinking, co-authored by Professor Christopher Hakala of Western New England College and me (at Ithaca College), explores the fascinating field of cognitive psychology, a discipline focused on the processes by which people learn, solve problems, and display intelligence. Cognitive psychology is a fascinating field that explores how we absorb information, integrate it, and then act on it.

In *Developmental Psychology*, Professor Lynn Shelley of Westfield State University addresses the very broad area of psychology that examines how people develop and change from the moment of conception through old age. Dr. Shelley's detailed and compelling explanation includes a focus on how maturation and environment play a part in shaping how each individual grows, evolves, and changes.

In *Personality and Abnormal Psychology*, Professor Janet Carlson of the Buros Center for Testing at the University of Nebraska (Lincoln) addresses various dimensions of personality, highlighting processes that influence normal and abnormal facets of personality. Dr. Carlson also explains how psychologists study the fundamental nature of personality and how it unfolds.

The final volume in this series is *Social Psychology*. Co-authored by Professor Jeffrey Holmes of Ithaca College and Sheila Singh of Cornell University, this volume examines how our thoughts and behaviors emerge in connection with our interactions with other people. As the authors of this volume explain, changes in a person's social environment can lead to notable changes in the way that person thinks and behaves.

As editor of this series, I have had the opportunity to work with all of the authors who have contributed their expertise and insights to this project. During this collaborative process, I found that we have much in common. All of us have spent our careers pondering why people think and act the way they do. For every answer we come up with, we also develop new questions that are just as interesting and important. And we all agree that you cannot find a more interesting subject to study than psychology.

As you learn about psychology, we hope that the information in these seven volumes inspires the same fascination in you. We also hope that our explanations, illustrations, and narrative studies motivate you to continue studying why we humans are the way we are.

—Bernard C. Beins, Ph.D., Professor of Psychology,
Ithaca College, Series Editor

INTRODUCTION

Social Psychology is the study of how people's thoughts, feelings, and behaviors are affected by other people. Just as we react to others, our own behavior influences the thoughts, feelings, and behaviors of those around us. This complex cycle persists throughout our lives in countless ways. This book provides a brief introduction to the vast and fascinating field of social psychology. Although the information presented here is a relatively brief overview of the field, it provides a broad general introduction to the major areas of social psychological research. More than a century of such research has yielded a rich collection of findings about human behavior—many of which are quite surprising.

Chapter 1 highlights the major areas of research concerning group behavior. Being part of a group can affect a person's behavior in powerful ways—sometimes for the better but all too often for the worse. In the anonymity of groups, people sometimes commit heinous acts that they would never even consider when not acting as part of a group. On the other hand, and under certain conditions, being part of a group can also result in improvement in one's performance on various tasks. The opening chapter of this book will illustrate how groups affect individual behavior in numerous (and often unanticipated) ways.

In Chapter 2 we explore attitudes, something all people have about various areas of life. Social psychologists have concerned themselves with understanding where attitudes come from, how they change, and how they influence behavior. The area of attitude research has broad application within and beyond the field of psychology. Consider advertising, for example. The purpose of advertising is to influence our attitudes—with the assumption that changes in behavior will follow in ways that the advertisers desire. As Chapter 2 will illustrate, attitudes are influenced by many sources but are often surprisingly inconsistent with behavior. That is, what we think and how we feel often does not match what we do.

Chapter 3 outlines the concepts of conformity, compliance, and obedience. In this case we are looking at more than our internal thoughts about the world. When we conform, comply, or obey, it is our behavior that changes—whether or not our internal attitudes are affected. Research on these concepts is particularly fascinating because it illustrates how easily behavior can be influenced and directed by others. This area of social psychology frequently raises awareness that people very often underestimate the degree to which the environment and people around them control their behavior. In the most dramatic cases, people have committed horrific acts against innocent victims, simply because someone in authority told them to do so.

In Chapter 4 we examine stereotyping, prejudice, and discrimination. In simple terms, these concepts constitute different components of the same phenomenon. Stereotypes are reflected in our thought processes, prejudice reflects our emotional responses, and discrimination involves our behavior. Because stereotypes are intricately linked with our normal mental processes, countering them is exceptionally difficult. This in turn can affect emotion (prejudice) and can promote or support certain behavior (discrimination). Finding effective ways to combat prejudice and discrimination has been a central focus over much of the history of social psychology.

Chapter 5 introduces the subject of interpersonal relationships. Researchers have studied all types of relationships including friendships, family relationships, and romantic relationships. The findings consistently demonstrate that our relationships are affected by numerous factors, many of which we seldom consider. Sometimes research confirms our intuitions about human relationships, sometimes not. Sometimes it confirms what we would like to believe, sometimes not. One clear conclusion is that the quality of our relationships is associated with the quality of our lives in general. Another is that the absence of social ties can cause great harm.

In chapter 6, we look at human behavior at its best and worst. Prosocial behaviors are those that help other people. Antisocial behaviors are those that cause harm. Many researchers have attempted to understand the factors that make people help or hurt each other. The findings reflect the reality that any individual action by any individual human being is the culmination of countless prior learning and genetic influences. Research very effectively allows for a reasonably good understanding of general trends in behavior among groups of people, but it is often less effective in helping us understand why specific events occur. This makes a complete and precise understanding of human behavior challenging, but it also makes the study of psychology that much more fascinating.

CHAPTER 1

BEHAVIOR IN GROUPS

Understanding how people behave differently when they are members of groups than they do when they are alone is a cornerstone of social psychology. Many decades of research have demonstrated that the presence and actions of those around us can have a profound impact on what we think, feel, and do.

DEFINITION OF A GROUP

Most people know what they mean when they refer to a **group**. They simply mean that several people are together in the same place. This seems rather obvious, but social psychologists typically apply a more specific definition. This is important because the influence that others have on us depends on a number of specific factors. For example, the strength and nature of group influence on individual behavior is affected by the number of people in the group, the level of personal identification between group members, and numerous other characteristics. Thus, many years of research have allowed social psychologists to develop a refined understanding of how our behavior may be different— sometimes radically so— when we act as members of a group rather than as individuals.

Consider the times when you have been part of a group. You might think of times when you were in a classroom, a club meeting, or out with friends. In such cases you may know the other members of the group quite well, and your personal interests may be intertwined with theirs. If you think harder you may remember times that you were waiting in line to buy something or watching an

Unlike in a classroom or a club meeting, you would not share an "interdependence of fate" with the strangers you meet while waiting in a line. *(Edal Anton Lefterov. Wikipedia)*

event on the street, such as workers constructing a building. In the latter cases you were among a group of people but you probably did not know most of them, nor did you feel any strong commitment to that group.

One of the earliest investigators of group influences on individual behavior was Kurt Lewin. He suggested that several individuals in the same place at the same time would not become a group in the psychological sense until they share what he called an "interdependence of fate." What Lewin meant by this was that something binds individuals in a group together psychologically so the interests of each person somehow become interdependent.

To understand how this comes about and how multiple individuals together do not necessarily constitute a group, imagine that you are standing on a city street watching as a building is being constructed. You would probably feel little connection with the people around you and little motivation to remain once your personal objectives (watching construction) have been satisfied. However, imagine that as you are about to leave the area to go on with your day, you and those around you hear a crash as two cars collide on the street nearby. It is at that moment that psychologists would say that you have become part of a group. Almost instantaneously you would likely feel a variety of social pressures that would motivate your behavior. You might feel compelled to assist the victims of the accident; you might take a leadership role and attempt to direct others to perform various tasks; you might feel confusion when it is not clear whether you should intervene or even when it is appropriate for you to leave. Any of these reactions would be a factor of the actions of those around you and your past experiences as a member of groups.

GROUP DEVELOPMENT

There are many types of groups and they differ in a variety of ways. Sometimes we choose to join a particular group and sometimes membership is imposed with little input from us. You are probably a member of many different groups of which you chose to be a part. These might include athletic teams, school clubs, and groups of friends. It is also likely that you are a part of groups that you did not join voluntarily. People do not choose who their family members will be, nor do they generally choose their particular high school. Group size also varies. You are probably a member of some large groups (such as an entire high school class), but you also may be part of small groups (such as clubs and teams). Finally, groups differ in their duration. Family members typically remain part of the same group for many years, whereas other groups have a much more limited lifespan (such as a group what witnesses an accident while waiting in a line). The size, the degree to which membership is voluntary, and the expected lifespan of a particular group often influence individual behavior within the group and also the degree to which each member feels connected with the larger group identity.

People choose to join groups for a variety of reasons, and human beings often appear to have a basic need to be part of groups—a need that may be based in human evolution where members of groups were simply more likely to survive and produce offspring than humans who were less socially oriented. Especially in more primitive surroundings such as those in which our distant ancestors lived, group membership would provide increased protection from environmental threats as well as shared responsibility for acquiring food. This evolved preference for avoiding isolation persists in modern society, where social interaction provides a sense of belongingness and promotes mental health. Indeed, one of the cruelest punishments inflicted on prison inmates is confinement in isolation cells where contact with other people is greatly restricted or even eliminated entirely. Such treatment often leads to rapid and dramatic psychological consequences such as extreme anxiety, depression, and even delusions and hallucinations. Fortunately most of us will never experience the extreme social deprivation faced by those in isolation cells. Nonetheless, most of us have probably experienced the value of group membership and can understand the negative emotions that accompany feelings of being left out of groups.

Group development involves a period of adjustment as the members become acquainted and begin to learn the rules of the group. There are many perspectives on how this process occurs, but the best known was developed by Bruce Tuckman. Tuckman identified several stages that he said groups progress through during their existence. During the Forming stage, initial relationships develop and members test the boundaries of the group; in the Storming stage, members begin to exert individual influence on the group, which often leads to conflict; in the Norming stage, much of the earlier conflict is resolved as members learn their roles and begin to identify with the group; finally, Performing is characterized by members applying their new roles toward successful completion of group tasks. Although there are more complex models of group development and functioning, Tuckman's model provides a useful framework for understanding group processes.

Established groups have a number of characteristics that greatly influence the behavior of members. Most groups have members who fulfill different roles. One example of this is when a member takes on leadership responsibilities. The leadership role may be rather informal, as is often the case within a group of friends. Alternatively, the role may be formalized, as in cases where the leader

Many high school and college students greatly exaggerate the degree of alcohol use among their peers. *(Shutterstock)*

Social Norming

Some researchers have attempted to reduce problematic behaviors—particularly alcohol abuse—by altering perceived social norms. One example of this is efforts aimed at reducing the level of alcohol consumption among students. Many high school and college students greatly exaggerate the degree of alcohol use among their peers, believing that "everyone does it." The reasons for this are complex but there are two particularly important factors. The first is that people who drink alcohol tend to spend a great deal of their time with other people who drink. Second, the perception that alcohol consumption is the norm makes it less likely that young people who do not drink will make this fact known. These two factors contribute to a shared perception that alcohol use is far more common than it is. Advocates of social norming attempt to replace such exaggerations with more accurate social norms by educating young people about real alcohol consumption rates. That is, they replace perceived norms with actual behavioral data in order to shift the norms in a more realistic direction. Evaluations of the social norming approach to behavior change have been mixed and despite the important objectives of such programs, it is not clear that simply informing people of objective data on the frequency of a particular behavior will be sufficient to alter powerful existing social norms.

carries a title such as teacher or chairperson. Whether formally recognized or not, a member's role in the group will affect the behavior of that member as well as that of other participants.

Groups also have norms for appropriate behavior. **Norms** are simply guidelines that steer members' behavior in particular directions. Norms can be explicit, as is the case when members must wear a uniform. However, norms are not always so clearly mandated, and you can probably remember times when you struggled to figure out how to behave in a particular group. Failure to adhere to a group's norms often results in uncomfortable social consequences as other group members respond negatively to violation of their standards.

Finally, groups have varying degrees of **cohesiveness**. This refers to the degree to which group members feel close ties and commitment to the group's identity. Groups with high levels of cohesiveness tend to promote conformity among members, as pressures toward group solidarity prohibit individuals from expressing dissenting opinions. Cohesiveness is sometimes helpful, as it tends to enhance group performance on various tasks; it can also be harmful, however, as it often leads to the suppression of original thought and alternative viewpoints.

DEINDIVIDUATION

What makes people commit acts—sometimes destructive, violent, and immoral acts—when they are part of a group when those same people would never engage in such behaviors on their own? An important concept to consider when analyzing this question is the phenomenon of **deindividuation**. Beginning in the 1950s, researchers began investigating how people's levels of self-awareness and individual identity change when they become part of a group. Early research suggested that activating a group identity often leads individual members to abandon their own personal morals and values and to adopt the values, morals, and behaviors mandated by the group. The term *deindividuation* refers to this loss of individual identity in favor of group identity.

One of the most important observations concerning deindividuation is that people are less likely to help someone in distress when there are other people present. Research on this phenomenon began in earnest in the 1960s, following a highly publicized crime in New York City. The incident involved a young woman named Kitty Genovese, who was brutally attacked and ultimately murdered outside her apartment building. Tragic as this event was, the element that brought it to the attention of social psychologists was initial reports that dozens of people heard Genovese scream for help during the attack, which lasted approximately half an hour. Although continued investigation of the crime suggested that not every nearby witness was as complacent as first reported, the general reluctance to offer assistance to someone so clearly in need of help spurred researchers to examine what came to be known as the **bystander effect**.

If you knew your car was going to break down and that you would need to rely on strangers for assistance, would you rather your car failed on a crowded interstate highway or on a rural road with little traffic? Intuition may tell you that your chances of receiving assistance would be greater on the highway, simply because there are many more drivers around so the odds of someone stopping to help are more in your favor. However, research on deindividuation and the related bystander effect suggest just the opposite. When a situation requires action and many people are present, the perceived responsibility each individual feels is divided among the many people. If you have ever seen a stranded motorist, for example, you may have told yourself that someone else would help. What we do not always recognize in the moment is that all of the other motorists are in the same situation and are likely telling themselves the very same thing. The net result is often that no one offers assistance.

In an early study of the bystander effect conducted in 1968, John Darley and Bibb Latane tested college students who thought they were participating in research about college life. The research actually began while they were discussing the supposed research topic with others over an intercom system. The participant heard sounds over the intercom indicating that another participant

Kitty Genovese *(NY Daily News Archive/Getty)*

was having a seizure. In cases where a participant believed he or she was the only one aware of the seizure, the vast majority reported that an emergency was occurring. However when participants believed that others were also aware of the seizure, fewer than 1 in 3 reported the emergency. Numerous subsequent studies yielded similar results but also revealed that observers who are part of groups are generally not simply indifferent to others' suffering. Instead their tendency to offer assistance is suppressed by the uncertainty of the situation and the absence of clear roles for taking responsibility. As may have been the case in your imagined experience observing someone stranded due to car trouble,

Rioting

Group effects not only promote inaction when action is called for, they can also lead people to commit overtly destructive acts. People rioting and destroying property after their favorite sports team wins an important game provides a noteworthy example. Most members of such rioting groups would never break windows, burn automobiles, or otherwise damage property when going about their everyday lives. In fact, in another setting, most would probably condemn such acts. Nonetheless, the situational pressures imposed by a group become too powerful and people's behavior ceases to reflect their individual values. As individual identity and morality are put on hold and a group identity is adopted, the person may engage in acts that observers outside the group find abhorrent.

Riot in Moldova after the 2009 parliamentary elections. *(Wikipedia. Courtesy of VargaA)*

participants in these studies simply are not sure whether intervention is appropriate and are immobilized by their uncertainty.

GROUP PERFORMANCE
Social Loafing

You can probably recall many times in your life when you had to cooperate with others to perform a task. You may have worked with your family to clean the house or rake leaves, and you may have worked with peers on projects required for school. In such cases, completion of the task results from a combination of the efforts of all group members. Naturally the quality of the group's performance would be maximized if all members worked as hard as they could on the task. However if you have ever worked on group projects with classmates, you are probably quite aware that this is not always what happens.

Social loafing means that people often do not work as hard when they are members of a group than they do when working individually, and research on this phenomenon goes back more that 100 years. What was probably the first formal study of social loafing was conducted by an engineer rather than a psychologist. Max Ringelmann had people perform the simple task of pulling on a rope as hard as they could. He observed that people pulled harder when they were working alone than they did when someone else was pulling with them. Presumably the participants did not get stronger when they were by themselves, they simply expended more effort. Many researchers over the past century have replicated this study using many different tasks, such as cheering as loudly as possible or making financial donations. The findings are remarkably consistent: As the size of a group increases, the effort exerted by individual group members tends to decrease.

How might we explain the phenomenon of social loafing? One explanation is that in groups, people's individual efforts cannot be fully evaluated so they expend less effort because they feel they may not earn proper credit if they work harder. Expending less effort may also allow a person to feel protected from responsibility in case the group's performance is inadequate. It may also be the case that people working in groups actually anticipate that other members will not work hard so they reduce their own efforts to avoid the risk that the others will take advantage by earning credit for their work. These are just some of the explanations for lowered effort in groups, but psychologists have also identified factors that reduce the likelihood that social loafing will occur. Some of these factors are based in personality, such as one's level of motivation to perform well on tasks in general, and are therefore less subject to influence by others. Moreover, teachers and others who supervise group work can employ various strategies that reduce loafing. For example, they might minimize loafing by using small groups, helping group members to recognize why a task is important, and structuring the work so that each member's performance can be observed.

Social Inhibition and Social Facilitation

Try to remember a time when you were required to perform some task in front of others. You might have delivered a speech in front of your class or even in front of the entire school, or you may have demonstrated your singing, acting, or athletic talents in front of an audience. In recalling such an event, did it feel like the presence of others observing your behavior increased or decreased the quality of your performance? Did you feel that your performance was better when the big day came or did you wish afterwards that the audience could have seen your performances from earlier practice sessions? Social psychologists have found that the pressure we feel when others are present sometimes enhances our performance; in other cases, the pressure can make us perform poorly even though our ability is high.

The presence of others can have a powerful effect on individual performance when the individual's behavior, rather than that of the group as a whole, is the focus of attention. Whether this influence leads to an increase or decrease in the quality of performance depends largely on the nature of the task. **Social inhibition**, commonly referred to as choking, occurs when a person attempts a complex task but feels pressure from others to perform well. For example, world class figure skaters train for countless hours over many years so that they can perform their routines flawlessly. Despite this preparation, some skaters make costly mistakes when they must perform the routines in front of a large audience rather than during a quiet practice session.

Interestingly, effort and performance do not always suffer when a person is in the presence of others. A person's performance may actually improve when others are present, a phenomenon referred to as **social facilitation**. One type of situation that promotes improved performance is when the performer is not merely in the presence of others, but is also in direct competition with others. You may have experienced this if you have ever participated in athletic competitions. In one of the first studies on social facilitation, Norman Triplett compared bicycle riders' speed when racing against others with their speed when they were racing only against a clock. He found that riders were faster when competing against others. The comparison of social facilitation and social inhibition illustrates how the presence of others can serve to enhance or hinder individual performance depending on context.

Brainstorming

Imagine yourself sitting in a classroom when the teacher explains that the class must identify strategies to raise money for an upcoming class trip. The teacher explains that the objective is to think of as many strategies as possible and encourages the class to work together to "brainstorm" ideas. This approach is frequently used to produce ideas for solving problems or performing important tasks. In the above example, would you expect that people would produce more and better ideas working as a group or as individuals? Because conventional wisdom avers that "two heads are better than one," most people would probably expect that **brainstorming** within a group is more effective, but this is often not the case.

Our current concept of brainstorming was developed by Alex Osborn in 1957. Osborn worked in advertising and believed that people working in groups would work harder and produce more novel ideas than they would if working independently. His approach was to instruct group members to produce as many ideas as possible and to refrain from criticizing any idea that any group member presented. He assumed that this strategy would inspire a kind of group energy that would make group productivity greater than what could be accomplished by individuals. Given what you have read about social loafing, you might already be suspicious of Osborn's views. In fact, numerous studies confirm that people working in groups actually produce fewer new ideas, and moreover produce ideas of lesser quality, than people working by themselves. Such conclusions seem to contradict our common sense about how people work, but popular opinion about brainstorming has been slow to change. Indeed the practice remains widely used and is commonly accepted as an effective approach to solving problems.

There are several reasons our common sense perception about brainstorming behavior is flawed, and there are related factors that help explain why people in groups often do not produce as many new ideas as we would expect. Some members of a group may be reluctant to express ideas because they fear being criticized by other members; others may censor themselves if they feel their ideas are inferior to those already produced. This reluctance may be especially likely for less outgoing members. Furthermore, a person's ideas may be forgotten while he or she waits as another member expresses thoughts. Finally, the tendency toward social loafing might lead otherwise highly motivated individuals to expend less effort in response to limited effort on the part of less motivated group members. Although there may be times when brainstorming is effective, a leader who wants a group to produce as many good ideas as possible needs to be keenly aware of the well-established limitations of the traditional brainstorming technique.

DECISION MAKING IN GROUPS
Group Polarization
Imagine you are a member of a sorority or fraternity and you join a committee charged with deciding what tasks prospective members must perform before joining this organization. The members of your committee have an array of

viewpoints on how severe the initiation process should be. As discussion among the committee members progresses, would you expect the group to begin leaning toward more lenient or more severe initiation rites? As the discussion below reveals, group interaction can influence decision making in unexpected ways.

James Stoner, who at the time of his now famous research was a student at the Massachusetts Institute of Technology, is often credited with being the first to study **group polarization** in decision making. Prior to 1961, when Stoner was conducting research for his master's thesis, conventional wisdom dictated that decisions made by groups or committees were likely to be more rational and conservative than decisions made by individuals. This wisdom was based on the logical assumption that pressure from the group would suppress more extreme individual perspectives and that the group would thus arrive at a decision representing the average initial viewpoint of the members. In rather stark contrast to this assumption, Stoner observed that the decision reached by a group is often more risky than a decision that might have been made by any one of the group's members had they been independently responsible for the choice. This phenomenon came to be known as **risky shift** and refers to the tendency of groups to shift toward less cautious choices after discussing an issue. Several studies that followed Stoner's thesis did indeed suggest that groups often make riskier decisions than individuals. In such studies, researchers would typically present participants with a problem scenario and ask each individual to explain how he or she thought the given situation should be handled. Participants would then discuss the issue with other participants, and the researchers would ask them to come to a group decision on the same question. The decision proposed by the group was often riskier than any of those proposed by individuals.

Like many research findings in psychology, the early results suggesting a tendency toward risky shift in group decision making presented an incomplete picture of how human beings function in various situations. Some studies began to yield results that contradicted the risky shift phenomenon and appeared to confirm the conventional wisdom that groups are more cautious than individuals. What soon became apparent is that group decisions are not always more risky, nor are they always more conservative. Researchers determined that group discussion tends to shift the group farther in the direction that its members already preferred. Therefore the term *risky shift* was replaced with the much more accurate term *group polarization* because it was found that group views tend to become more polarized than individual members' views. When a group tends to favor riskier options, discussion among the members promotes movement toward even greater risk. When the group is initially more cautious, discussion promotes even greater caution.

Interestingly, research on a whole variety of topics such as gambling risk, jury decision making, and racial prejudice suggests that group discussion leads viewpoints to become more extreme than initially reported. There have been many explanations for why this would occur. For one thing, group members may be exposed to new information during discussion, information that they were not aware of beforehand. Furthermore, such information would be provided by group members interested in influencing the group's perspective and would therefore be persuasive in nature. This would particularly explain why groups sometimes shift toward more extreme views.

Whatever the group's initial leaning, group discussion is likely to produce more arguments in favor of that leaning than against it. Based on the sheer number of arguments presented in favor of the group's perspective, members might begin to believe that the arguments countering this perspective are less viable than first thought, which would justify moving even farther away from them and even closer to the initially favored viewpoint. A related consequence of group discussion arises when individual members inevitably compare their views to those of other members. In this case, one may recognize that other members' views are similar to one's own but that some members' views are more extreme. This would change the individual's perception of group norms, and he or she may then express more extreme views to fit better with perceived majority expectations. This in turn would have similar effects on other members with less extreme views.

Groupthink

Often when a group of people must make a decision on some important issue, there is great pressure to come to an agreement quickly and avoid dissent. In 1972, Irving Janis identified a phenomenon he called **groupthink**, a phenomenon strongly related to this pressure. Janis pointed to several important events in United States history that illustrate the dangers that groupthink poses to effective decision making. As one such example, Janis cited the United States' misguided invasion of Cuba in 1961, an event which came to be known as the Bay of Pigs invasion. Prior to the invasion, President John F. Kennedy brought together several advisers who were to help him make the decision about whether or not to invade Cuba. The belief among the advisers was that the invasion would trigger a revolution among Cuban citizens, which would ultimately lead to the ouster of Cuban leader Fidel Castro. The meetings between President Kennedy and his advisers were lengthy and detailed, but the pressures imposed by groupthink led the leaders to ignore many important details that would have alerted them to the inevitable failure of the proposed invasion.

According to Janis, several conditions of group decision making are likely to promote groupthink. First, groupthink is likely when a group is high in cohesiveness. Cohesiveness refers to the degree to which group members identify with the group and feel close to the other members. Second, groupthink is likely when the group has a single strong leader, and the group members are homogenous—that is, similar to each other and having similar views on the issue at hand. It is under these conditions, and if a group is under pressure to come to a decision involving stressful circumstances, that groupthink is most likely to surface.

Cover of *Life* magazine after the Bay of Pigs invasion. *(Photo by Sanford Kossin/Time and Life Pictures/Getty)*

Groupthink often results in poor decision making. Because the group members share similar views, are subject to (or subordinate to) a strong leader whose perspective is often consistent with that of the members, and identify strongly with the group as a whole, the decisions reached are often unrealistic. By extension, actions based on such decisions are likely to fail. The absence of dissent within the group may instill in members the perception that agreement would be widespread outside the group as well. As the perception of agreement grows stronger, individual members become less likely to express doubts about a proposed course of action, further increasing the perception that agreement is unanimous and enhances the group's sense of certainty. When a decision is ultimately reached, it is likely to reflect an incomplete evaluation of options and risks.

In the case of the Bay of Pigs invasion, groupthink likely prevented the President and his advisers from recognizing what were later considered obvious flaws in strategy and unrealistic assumptions concerning the anticipated response of the Cuban people. But groupthink is not limited to military decisions made by groups of politicians. It can emerge anytime a relatively uniform group of people with a strong leader must make important decisions.

Fortunately there are steps that conscientious group leaders can take to minimize the impact of groupthink on group decision making. Janis proposed that members be told to offer dissenting views or to play devil's advocate, that leaders allow the discussion to proceed before offering their own views, that groups not limit themselves to insiders who are likely to share the same perspectives, and that the most important decisions be allocated independently to more than one group to see if different groups arrive at similar conclusions. Although the principles of groupthink appeal to common sense and are relatively easy to comprehend, research on the phenomenon is notoriously incomplete because of the difficulty involved in creating research groups that operate under conditions paralleling those faced by real-life groups. Because of this difficulty, most research on groupthink consists of historical anecdotes and case studies that are intuitively satisfying but may not represent a complete picture of the processes involved.

Social Dilemmas

Another concept relevant to decision making in groups is that of **social dilemmas**. Like group polarization effects, social dilemmas exist when a decision must be made in a group context. The two concepts, however, differ significantly in impact, both on the group and on individual members within the group. Group polarization occurs when several people must discuss a topic and render a decision or viewpoint that is generally agreed upon by everyone. In other words, the decision belongs to the group as a whole. In the case of social dilemmas, the decision belongs to the individual. It is made by a person who is part of a group, but that person must decide whether to prioritize his or her own needs over the needs of the group. Social dilemmas involve decisions about whether to sacrifice some aspect of one's individual interests for the greater good.

For example, picture yourself having dinner at a restaurant with a group of friends. As the end of the meal approaches, someone suggests that the bill be split evenly rather than calculating individual charges. You may look around silently wondering why you should pay for part of a meal for someone who ordered a more expensive dish. Alternatively, you may consider ordering an expensive dessert knowing that the cost will be divided among those present and therefore your individual cost will be low. If you choose to order the dessert, you will experience short-term gain when you acquire a tasty treat for minimal expense. However, such behavior will have consequences for group resources—especially if all group members take the same approach. Seeking short-term individual advantage might also harm your long-term relationships with your friends.

When you face a social dilemma you must essentially decide whether to cooperate with others or to compete with them. Researchers have studied the ways in which people evaluate and resolve such dilemmas, and what conditions determine whether someone is likely to cooperate or compete. The most famous research procedure for studying social dilemmas is known as the "prisoner's dilemma." Imagine you are a research participant playing the role of someone accused of committing a crime with the help of a partner. The police have evidence of your involvement, and the dilemma you face is whether to confess to planning the crime. You are not permitted to speak with your co-defendant, but you are told that if both you and your partner confess you will each serve a prison sentence of 2 years. If neither of you confesses you will each serve a 3 year sentence. Most importantly, if only one of you confesses the person admitting guilt will serve 4 years whereas the other will serve only 1 year. In such a case, producing the best outcome for yourself (the shortest sentence) means both deciding whether to cooperate or compete *and* anticipating what your partner is likely to do.

Research using the prisoner's dilemma has been extensive and has yielded interesting findings. Studies often include repeating the exercise with the same participants so researchers can observe not only people's initial tendencies, but also their responses after becoming aware of a partner's responses during earlier trials. Many people begin with a cooperative approach but shift to a tit-for-tat approach as time goes on. That is, they base their responses on a partner's previous behavior. If their partner cooperated on the previous trial, they are likely to cooperate during the next round. In real life, such a tendency may in fact help groups to remain stable and congenial. You probably know people who seem always to be competitive. Although competition is certainly not in itself a bad thing, excessive competition and inability to cooperate will likely have a negative effect on group members' ability to get along. Many factors affect how one will respond to social dilemmas. These include individual personality characteristics, competitive orientation, cultural experiences, and gender; they also include situational characteristics, such as whether the group is small or large, and whether there are group norms promoting a particular response.

SUMMARY

This chapter has addressed some of the ways that the presence of others influences our behavior. Being part of a group requires more than simply being in the presence of others; it requires that the interests or identities of those present are somehow linked. Groups can enhance our performance on tasks, but they can also hinder our performance and keep us from intervening when action is appropriate. A common sense view of the influence of groups is often inaccurate. We might expect that groups are likely to produce more ideas and make better decisions than individuals, but research demonstrates that the opposite is often true. Groups serve important functions and offer us a sense of belongingness and identity. Under certain circumstances however, group influence can bring out the worst in us.

Further Reading

Latane, Bibb, and John M. Darley. *The Unresponsive Bystander: Why Doesn't He Help?* New York: Meredith, 1970.

Parks, Craig D., and Lawrence J. Sanna. *Group Performance and Interaction*. Boulder, Colo.: Westview Press, 1999.

Tuckman, Bruce W. "Developmental Sequence in Small Groups." *Psychological Bulletin* 63, no. 2 (Jun 1965): 384–399.

CHAPTER 2

ATTITUDES AND ATTITUDE CHANGE

Are you in favor of the death penalty? Do you like reading? Do you respect professional athletes? Do you look forward to speaking to groups? Do you like Brussels sprouts? Your responses to these and countless other questions reveal something about your attitudes. As you probably already know, all people have attitudes about all kinds of things. **Attitudes** are our tendencies to respond in particular ways to particular people, groups, objects, or situations. They can be very positive or very negative, but usually they fall somewhere in between. For example, some people favor the death penalty and some oppose it, but most do not have extreme views either way. Students with strong attitudes about school may either dislike academic work or enjoy it very much, but most probably have some classes they like and some they do not. In this chapter we examine various components that comprise the attitudes that psychologists study, strategies that people use to influence our attitudes, and how our behavior is often surprisingly inconsistent with our attitudes.

COMPONENTS OF ATTITUDES

Although most of us think of an attitude as a single entity, any particular attitude may consist of a number of components. The first of these is the cognitive component, which refers to thoughts and beliefs about the target of an attitude. If you have an attitude about professional athletes, the cognitive component might contain knowledge that athletes work hard, have great physical strength, travel frequently, and make a great deal of money. The cognitive component also contains value judgments based partly on what you know and partly on your beliefs. You may, for example, perceive professional athletes as arrogant and overpaid or generous and compassionate. The cognitive features of attitudes are shaped by your past learning and experiences. Differing experiences and knowledge are part of the reason that different people have different attitudes about the same thing.

A second component of attitude is the affective component. When psychologists use the word *affect*, they are referring to mood or emotion. In the case of attitudes, the affective component refers to the emotions that we associate with various people or situations. If you have a positive attitude about public speaking, you may experience happiness and excitement when you are assigned the task of presenting something to a group. For those whose attitude about public speaking is negative, the assignment may trigger fear and anxiety.

The third component of attitude is the behavioral component, which includes the intention(s) to respond in particular ways to the target of a given attitude. If you have a positive attitude toward a politician, the behavioral component might include your intention to vote for that person. If you have a positive attitude toward recycling, the behavioral component might include your intention to take cans and bottles to recycling points rather than discarding them in the trash.

The cognitive, affective, and behavioral components of attitudes often interact collectively to determine our experiences. At other times only one or two of these components may be operating. It seems logical to assume that the cognitive component of an attitude comes first and that emotions and behaviors are the natural end products of what we know about something. After all, don't we first learn the facts about something and then decide how we feel and how we should act? But as you will see later in this chapter, the cognitive component of an attitude does not always rule. For one thing, the knowledge and beliefs that comprise the cognitive component are often inaccurate or incomplete. For this and other reasons, there are times when the cognitive, affective, and behavioral components are at odds with each other.

WHERE DO OUR ATTITUDES COME FROM?

We do not always know where our attitudes come from. If you are opposed to the death penalty, do you remember an experience that led you to possess that view? More often than not, we cannot identify a specific event that explains our general attitude about something. Nonetheless, it is probably safe to assume that all of our attitudes reflect our past experiences in some way. No one is born a Democrat or a Republican, nor is anyone a born fan of sports, music, or school. The affinity for (or dislike of) a particular political party or a particular musical instrument or sport emerges as a result of our experiences. In other words, the attitude is learned. Social psychologists have identified

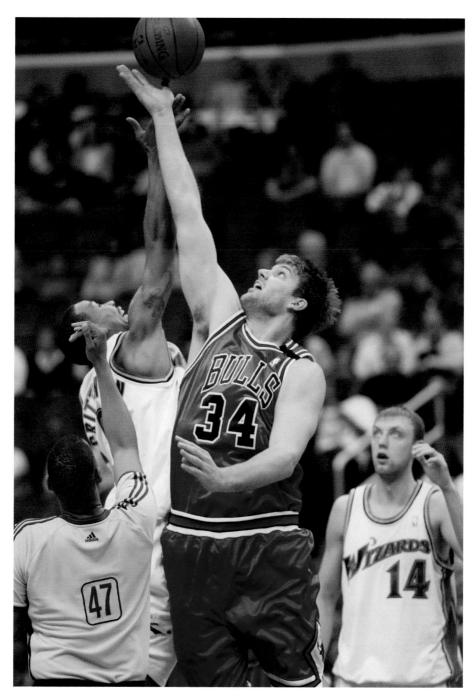

The cognitive component of an attitude about professional athletes might include knowledge that these athletes work hard and might also include value judgments, such as a belief that they are overpaid and arrogant. *(Keith Allison. Wikipedia)*

a number of ways in which attitudes are learned. Many of these reflect basic learning principles that psychologists have studied for at least a century.

It is probably no surprise to most people that we acquire many of our attitudes through **observational learning**. This type of learning takes place when we watch and imitate other people. Early in life, we learn many attitudes by watching our parents and other adults. Our social attitudes, views about how to treat others, and even many of our interests, are likely to coincide with those of our parents. This is not to say that parents and their children always (or even usually) agree. But if you have a positive attitude about sports or you feel that everyone deserves to be treated well, it is likely that you can recall a close family member or friend early in life who had (and expressed) a similar attitude. As we get a little older, we acquire attitudes from a greater range of influential people, including friends and teachers, as well as more distant figures, such as musicians and movie stars. Of course, others learn attitudes from us as well. If you tell a friend how much you enjoyed your psychology class, your friend is more likely to have a positive attitude about psychology and may be more likely to take a psychology course as well.

Other types of learning can also affect the development of attitudes. If you have studied other areas of psychology you have probably heard the terms "classical conditioning" and "operant conditioning." **Classical conditioning** is most associated with the work of Ivan Pavlov and addresses how people learn associations between things that were not previously linked. In his famous work, Pavlov observed that when a bell was rung each time food was presented to the dogs in his physiology laboratory, the dogs soon began to salivate as soon as the bell was rung, even if no food was present. The dogs had acquired a conditioned association between the bell and the food, so they responded to the bell as if food were being delivered.

Although deceptively simple, the principles of classical conditioning are relevant to human attitudes and are especially useful for understanding how the affective or emotional components of attitudes can be learned so quickly and still be very powerful and pervasive. Anyone with a taste aversion to a particular food will understand the power of classical conditioning. Many taste aversions develop rapidly when a person experiences a serious stomach illness soon after eating. If you eat artichokes and become ill soon afterwards, you may develop a learned association between artichokes and the unpleasant symptoms of the illness. This association may be so strong that just thinking about artichokes makes you nauseous.

Interestingly, such associations do not always have any real causal connection. It may be that you were eating artichokes when you were already ill from some other cause (perhaps a stomach virus) but not yet experiencing symptoms related to that illness. Thus, the artichokes you currently despise had nothing to do with the discomforts of the stomach ailment. You would have been sick anyway, and your aversion to artichokes is accidental rather than causative. Knowing this seldom does much to reduce the aversion. And as this example illustrates, a lifelong attitude can be triggered by a single experience.

Advertisers often use classical conditioning principles and strategies. As they develop advertising campaigns, their objective is to create an association in the minds of potential customers between the product being advertised and the positive feelings evoked by some other stimulus. A soft drink company, for example, may develop a television commercial or other advertisement that features attractive people enjoying the company's beverages. It doesn't hurt that the beautiful people always appear to be having a fantastic time while consuming the product. The company is betting that through repeated presentation of this product, together with a stimulus that already elicits positive feelings (attractive people), the product will eventually come to elicit positive feelings as well.

A third type of learning that helps explain attitude development is **operant conditioning**. In this type of learning, studied most famously by B.F. Skinner, behavior comes to be controlled by its consequences. If we engage in a given

Supermodel Cindy Crawford drinks a Pepsi. What associations does the ad evoke? *(Photo courtesy of Pepsi/Getty)*

behavior and the outcome is positive (a reward or other reinforcement), we are more likely to engage in that behavior again. On the other hand, if the outcome of a given behavior is some negative consequence (for example, punishment or reprimand), we are less likely to behave that way again. Keep in mind, however, that all kinds of things can be reinforcing. When we do well we might get something tangible (such as a trophy, a plaque, or a raise) or something intangible (such as a complement or a pat on the back). In social interaction, intangible rewards and punishments are the norm. Friends are not likely to give you a dollar or a piece of candy when they like your shirt, but a flattering look or comment is likely to encourage you to wear that shirt again.

When it comes to attitudes, the rewards and punishments that others dole out can be quite influential. If you tell your friend about a band that you like and he or she responds, "those guys are great," it is likely to strengthen your positive attitude about that band. If, however, your friend expresses dislike for the band, your own attitude toward that band may become less positive. This is not to imply that our attitudes are so flexible that they can be dramatically altered or erased by a single comment from someone else. However, disagreement from others amounts to a type of social punishment that can gradually change our attitude about something. In contrast, someone agreeing with us is socially reinforcing, and we tend to persist with things that earn reinforcement from others. One of the reasons that our attitudes become so strongly entrenched is that we all tend to interact with people who have similar views. It is unusual to see a staunch Democrat attend a Republican committee meeting to hear what the opposition has to say. The result of surrounding ourselves with like-minded people is that our attitudes often are reinforced more than they are punished.

Sources of Attitudes

Many types of learning play a role in the development of attitudes. In fact, a single attitude may actually be traced to a variety of learning experiences. Imagine you have a positive attitude about a particular fast food restaurant. Did observational learning play a role because your friend told you that it was a great place to eat? Was classical conditioning involved as you sat outside the restaurant one day and enjoyable smells of food being cooked surrounded you, thus causing an association between the restaurant and a pleasurable sensation? Was operant conditioning a factor because you ate at the restaurant when no other options were available but then enjoyed an amazing meal that reinforced your decision to eat there? Regardless of the attitude, it was likely shaped by a host of past experiences.

THE ATTITUDE-BEHAVIOR CONNECTION

How would you respond if someone asked you whether your behavior is always consistent with your attitudes? You probably have positive attitudes toward many products, but do you purchase every product that elicits such attitudes? You may believe that it is important to recycle materials to protect the environment, but does this attitude always get translated into a behavior when you have the opportunity to recycle something? If you have a positive attitude about recycling but you throw your soda can into the trash, your behavior is inconsistent with your attitude. Such inconsistency is surprisingly common, and it occurs because attitudes simply represent generalized tendencies. In contrast, behavior is affected by the demands and limitations of the immediate situation. You may believe that recycling is important, but your decision about whether to recycle any particular item is affected by many other factors, such as convenience (recycling may require you to carry the can with you when there is a trash can nearby) or mood (you may have had a bad day so you are less attuned to your usual ideals). Immediate situational constraints often prevent our behavior from following our attitudes.

Two researchers, Icek Ajzen and Martin Fishbein, reviewed many decades of research on the link between attitudes and behavior. They explained that early research in social psychology seemed to show that people's attitudes did in fact predict what they would do in specific situations, but that researchers soon began to recognize that what people reported about their attitudes was often very different from how they behaved in specific situations—so much so that many researchers questioned whether research on people's reported attitudes had any real value in understanding behavior. Fortunately, perseverance and improvements in the ways that attitudes are measured helped researchers to better understand the complexity and relevance of attitudes.

Research on attitudes has produced some general patterns that help to clarify why they do not always predict what people will actually do. First, attitudes tend to predict single behaviors rather poorly, but they predict behavior over time quite well. If you have a positive attitude about recycling, there may be times when you do not recycle but, in general, you will recycle items far more frequently than someone who does not have a positive attitude about recycling. A person's behavior is also more likely to reflect his or her attitude when the attitude is strong and easily accessible. We have attitudes about a whole variety of things, but these attitudes are not equal in strength or in how easily they come to mind. You may feel strongly that recycling is important, so you recycle nearly all of your trash. In contrast, your friend may agree with you that recycling is important but her attitude on this subject may not be as strong, so she recycles less frequently. Attitudes predict what behaviors we are likely to engage in over time, but in any specific situation there may be other factors that override them.

Measuring Attitudes

Researchers have most commonly measured attitudes using relatively straight-forward surveys or questionnaires. Although surveys can be a useful method for collecting large quantities of information very efficiently, their effectiveness requires that respondents provide accurate, honest information. Although most people who complete surveys probably try to provide accurate information, there can be subtle pressure to present oneself in a positive light. Such pressure, known as social desirability, can vary from person to person and across situations. For example, imagine yourself completing a questionnaire assessing your attitudes about alcohol consumption. Is it possible that your responses might change somewhat depending on who was sitting next to you or who you thought might see your responses? Many topics of interest to attitude research-ers have the potential to elicit socially desirable responding. Because of con-cerns about the effects of such responding, some researchers have begun using **implicit attitude tests**. These tests attempt to bypass people's conscious control of their responses by requiring them to quickly categorize objects. This process reveals how closely associated various concepts are in a person's mem-ory. Because the person must respond rapidly, he or she is less able to deliber-ately censor or manipulate responses in a particular way. Implicit techniques are useful in some contexts, but surveys remain by far the most common strategy for measuring attitudes.

PERSUASION

Persuasion occurs when a person's attitude about something is altered because of the influence of someone else. There are many situations where others try to change our attitudes (and conversely, when we try to influence others). Adver-tisers seek to control our attitudes about their products; politicians and activ-ists try to influence our social, political, and economic attitudes; and people in our everyday lives routinely try to influence what we think and believe. Social psychologists have identified three critical components of persuasive com-munication. The source of the persuasive information is the person who actu-ally communicates with others; the message is the information itself; and the receiver is the person who is the target of the communication. Therefore per-suasion involves a specific source person using a specific message in an attempt to change the receiver's attitude. Each of these three factors plays an important role in determining whether persuasion is likely to be effective.

The Source

What characteristics do some people have that enhance their ability to persuade others? You have probably noticed that advertisers tend to hire people who are famous or good looking (or both) to help them shape people's attitudes about their products. They also look for representatives who are likely to be trusted by those who hear the message. If persuasion were all about the quality of communication, the characteristics of the person delivering the message would be irrelevant. In fact, there are many characteristics that tend to enhance the effectiveness of the source of persuasive communication. These characteristics fall into two broad categories. The first category is likeability, which simply refers to whether we feel positively toward someone. We are far more likely to be persuaded by a message that is delivered by someone we like rather than one delivered by someone we dislike.

There are many reasons why we might find a source to be likable. For example, we tend to like people who are physically attractive. Much research indicates that people attribute all kinds of positive psychological characteristics to people who are good-looking. It's as if we believe that nothing bad could come in so attractive a package. Further, the activation of these positive expectations often makes us experience pleasant feelings when we look at attractive people. With respect to persuasion, the positive feelings toward the source become associated in our minds with the message or product that the source is peddling.

Many advertisers are convinced that physical attractiveness is a critical component of persuasive communication, but the research on this has been somewhat inconclusive. Sometimes attractiveness seems to make a difference and sometimes not. One researcher, Shelly Chaiken, observed that much of the research on the effects of attractiveness in persuasive communication took place in laboratories rather than in field settings where real-life interactions occur. Although laboratory research is critical because it allows researchers to isolate individual factors that play a role in persuasion, the unnatural setting may affect the ways that people respond. Chaiken therefore trained college students—some physically attractive and some not—to approach other students on campus with a persuasive message. The persuaders attempted to convince other students to sign a petition prohibiting the campus dining hall from serving meat at breakfast or lunch. Chaiken's results showed that attractive persuaders were more effective than unattractive persuaders. However, Chaiken identified several other characteristics besides physical appearance that distinguished the attractive persuaders from the unattractive persuaders. Attractive people spoke more rapidly and more fluently, they rated themselves as more persuasive and interesting, they reported higher SAT scores and grade point averages, and they were perceived by their targets as more friendly. Physical attractiveness was associated with persuasion, but Chaiken noted that this effect may be partially due to other characteristics that tend to coincide with being attractive.

Another factor contributing to a source's likeability is the degree to which we perceive some similarity between the source and ourselves. We tend to like people who share our interests, values, or identity. A study by researcher Paul Silva clearly illustrates that this is an important element of persuasion. Silva conducted two experiments in which college students read persuasive essays that they believed were written either by a student very similar to or quite different from themselves. The results showed that students who thought the source of the essay was similar to them were more likely to agree with the content of the message. Perhaps even more interesting was the nature of the essays Silva included in this study: persuasive essays that either gave receivers a choice about what to believe or told them what they must believe. Ordinarily, telling people that they must believe something causes what is known as reactance, which leads them to rebel against the message. Reactance occurred in Silva's study but only in cases where participants believed the source of the persuasion was different from them. When people thought the source was like them, they tended to be persuaded by the essay even when told they had no choice. Participants also felt that sources similar to them were more likeable and less coercive, even though the essays presented by dissimilar sources were identical in content and style.

Research such as that contributed by Paul Silva shows that we are more likely to be persuaded and less likely to ask any questions if we think the source of a message is similar to us. Such findings strike a chord when we consider strategies used by those seeking or holding public office. We like people who are similar to us, and the obvious corollary to this is that politicians who portray themselves as similar to their constituents are more likely to be elected than those who do not. When politicians emphasize to their constituents (or voters) that they are from the same town or share the same background or values, they are capitalizing on what socials psychologists know about human behavior. Not only is this likely to help them to get elected, it is also likely to minimize negative reactance to policies implemented once the candidate is in office.

The second characteristic that determines whether a source is likely to be believed is credibility. A source's credibility increases when we feel that source has some expertise on the topic being communicated. We often trust what experts say, especially when we know little about a topic or are not motivated to investigate a topic on our own. Some researchers have gone so far as to argue that we have an expertise heuristic in that our general rule of thumb is to trust people who refer to themselves as experts. Expertise may be genuine and supported by a person's credentials, education, experience, and intelligence. Sometimes, however, we perceive someone as an expert with very little evidence. Thus, we may be persuaded regardless of whether the source's expertise is legitimate.

As one example of how expertise can be persuasive, consider the case of expert witnesses who testify in court. Expert witnesses are generally hired by those on one side of a court case or the other because those hiring the experts believe the testimony will support their point of view. Often the opposing sides

False Expertise

In a famous television commercial from the 1980s, a soap opera actor whose television character was a physician was hired for a commercial advertising a type of medication. In the commercial the actor said, "I'm not a doctor but I play one on TV." He then went on to describe the benefits of the medication almost as if he had real medical expertise. The advertisers took advantage of the actor's well-known role and invoked his perceived expertise even though his medical credentials were clearly and admittedly artificial.

each hire their own experts to testify about the same issue. The result is that the attorneys for each side go to great lengths to chip away at the credibility of the opposition's expert witness. The attorneys know that this is one of the most effective ways to reduce the persuasiveness of a source's communication.

Another factor that influences whether we perceive a source as credible is trustworthiness. To be persuaded, we need to feel that the person delivering the persuasive message is someone who would tell the truth. Our beliefs about the source's motives play a significant role in whether we feel he or she is trustworthy. Interestingly, we tend to trust people more when they argue for something that will not be personally beneficial to them. In contrast, we often become suspicious of people who try to persuade us of something that will ultimately benefit them—in other words, people who have a vested interest in supporting a particular viewpoint and in convincing others to do the same.

For example, imagine hearing a city councilman explain why it is important for your town to allow a company to clear land to build a new superstore in your area. He notes that the new store will bring many jobs and will create an economic boom for your town. You trust that your councilman has expertise in these matters, and it sounds like there is no downside to allowing the company to build. Now imagine that you are watching the local news and you hear that the same councilman who was emphasizing the benefits of the new store and advocating for its construction also happens to own the land on which the store is to be built. If the company is given permission to build, it would purchase the land from the councilman for a large sum of money. It is quite likely that this news would change your opinion about the councilman's credibility and trustworthiness because his vested interest is rather obvious (i.e., the councilman was motivated less by a desire to help the town than by his personal financial interests).

Generally a persuasive source must be both likeable and credible to be effective. Imagine a person was trying to persuade you to change your attitude about something. The person may be very attractive and share your background, but if he or she appears to know nothing about the topic at hand, you may deem the source and the message as lacking in credibility. Alternatively, imagine a source that is very knowledgeable but seems to have nothing in common with you. In this case, the source is lacking in likeability. The most effective persuasive communicators know they need both high likeability and high credibility.

The Message

Another aspect of persuasive communication that is critically important is the persuasive message itself, and psychological research tells us a great deal about how message effects play a role in persuasion. One important element to consider is the structure of a persuasive message. If you wanted to change people's attitude about something, would you present only the positive aspects of your position or would you also acknowledge the downsides? Psychologists refer to these as one-sided versus two-sided arguments.

The example of the city councilman in the section above illustrates the use of a one-sided argument. The councilman presented only those pieces of information that supported his point of view. Aside from failing to disclose his vested interest in the land development, he neglected to discuss any potential negative consequences, such as traffic problems or environmental degradation. There are times when it is wise to use such a one-sided approach and times when it is better to present both sides and then illustrate how one point of view is superior to the other. One-sided messages are more effective when the audience has little or no knowledge about the issue. If the receivers of the persuasive message do not know that there is a downside to your position, why would you tell them? It would generally be detrimental to your position to provide them with information that scores points against your goals. One-sided messages are also useful when the audience already leans in favor of the source's point of view. In these cases, the persuader capitalizes on what the audience would like to believe and provides information aimed at shifting their attitudes further in the desired direction.

As you might guess, the targets of persuasive communication often do know something about the issues being communicated. In such a case, two-sided arguments are more effective. When the audience knows there are pros and cons to a particular issue, ignoring one side or the other will likely lead people to perceive the source as untrustworthy. They might then become suspicious of the source's motives, which can cause the persuasive message to backfire. Two-sided messages are also more effective when the targets of persuasion disagree with the source's point of view. When this is the case, presenting both sides validates the audience's point of view, thus reducing the likelihood that people will become defensive and ignore the message. The two-sided strategy also gives the persuader the opportunity to rebut opposing arguments, which may enhance the effectiveness of the attempted persuasion. Finally, presenting both sides may enhance the source's credibility with the audience, which is important for reasons discussed earlier in this chapter.

Another characteristic to consider with respect to persuasive messages is the use of fear. A famous example of this was an anti-drug television campaign. The commercials for this campaign showed a person with a very serious expression holding up an egg and saying, "This is your brain." The person would then crack the egg into a hot frying pan. As the egg quickly began to sizzle, he or she would then say, "This is your brain on drugs." The clear implication was that drugs fry your brain so you should stay away from them. Such fear appeals are thought provoking and they certainly stir emotion, but are they effective at persuading people to change their attitudes or behavior? Research shows that fear appeals can be effective but only under certain conditions. First, the message must actually generate fear in the audience. Some messages are clearly intended to frighten people but if they are so unrealistic or so disconnected from the audience's experiences that no fear is induced, they will not be effective for generating attitude change. Furthermore, the message must generate a sufficient level of fear. In most case, producing only a slight fear response is less effective than producing a greater level of fear.

One very surprising aspect of persuasive communication is that we tend to perceive messages as more true when we have heard them repeatedly. This is known as the validity effect and researchers have shown that it operates separately from actual evidence for a claim. In other words, we perceive a statement that we have heard repeatedly as more true than a statement we have heard less often or not at all—even when no evidence supporting the statement has been offered. This phenomenon is particularly insidious because we are usually unaware that it is occurring. When we shop at the supermarket and believe that one brand of soft drink is superior to another, we don't realize that our belief stems from hearing repeated commercials touting that particular brand. The validity effect even plays a role in political propaganda. A leader might make claims that initially sound absurd and that people generally know are not true. However as the leader makes the same claims repeatedly over time, people often increasingly believe that the statements are true. Although saying something is true does not make it true, it can make it seem true in people's minds.

Receiver

It is important to recognize that the characteristics of the person hearing a persuasive message also play a role in the effectiveness of persuasion. We tend to think that some people are more gullible or persuadable than others, and this is certainly true. However, most people are easily persuaded in some circumstances and not easily persuaded in others. Researchers have examined a

Subliminal Persuasion

In the 1950s, James Vicary set off a social firestorm when he claimed that presenting very brief images of food during a movie increased attendees' purchases at the snack bar. Vicary claimed to have successfully used **subliminal** persuasion to change behavior. Subliminal messages are those that are presented to us outside of our conscious awareness—usually through visual images that appear for fractions of a second so observers are unable to consciously detect them. Most research on subliminal persuasion points to two clear conclusions. First, people are sometimes able to detect visual images that are presented so quickly that the observer is unable to identify them. This becomes evident when the participant subsequently responds more quickly to images that are associated with the initial image. Second and perhaps more important, there is very little evidence that people's behavior can be significantly influenced by subliminal messages. That is, your brain may somehow process the message without your awareness, but there is little reason to believe that you will then act differently or purchase certain products because of the message. Indeed, Vicary eventually admitted that he had made up his data, and a replication of his purported study revealed no change in observers' purchasing behavior.

number of individual characteristics that play a role in people's responsiveness to persuasive communication. The findings from many studies on this subject are quite complex, and the influence of personal characteristics often depends on the characteristics of the source or the nature of the message. Rather than making someone more or less susceptible to persuasion in general, certain personality traits make people susceptible to certain types of persuasive communication. Two examples that illustrate this concept involve need for cognition and self-monitoring.

Need for cognition refers to the degree to which a person is motivated to engage in complex thinking. People who possess this characteristic tend to focus on the persuasive message and therefore respond well to quality arguments. In contrast, people who are low in the need for cognition tend to avoid expending effort on thinking and are therefore persuaded more easily by source characteristics such as attractiveness and credibility. Self-monitoring describes how much a person monitors his or her own behavior in social situations. People high in self-monitoring focus on adjusting their public behavior to fit immediate environmental demands. Therefore they are persuaded by messages that emphasize social norms or majority opinion. In contrast, those low in self-monitoring are less motivated to change their behavior to fit the situation. Such people are more easily persuaded by messages that emphasize adhering to personal values.

Elaboration Likelihood Model

Perhaps the best known model of persuasion that incorporates source, message, and receiver factors is the **Elaboration Likelihood Model** (ELM). This model was proposed in 1986 by Richard Petty and John Cacioppo and has been extensively studied in the years since. The ELM proposes that persuasive communication can travel along two different routes. When the central route is used, a person attends to the quality of a persuasive message. In other words, the receiver pays close attention to what is being said and evaluates the message critically. For example, you might be persuaded that a particular model car is of high quality because a person in a commercial reports that the car requires fewer service visits than other vehicles require. Here the message shows convincing evidence of the car's quality. When persuasion attempts utilize the peripheral route, the emphasis is placed on the characteristics of the source rather than the message. Here, your attitude about a car's quality might be affected by the fact that a famous race car driver appeared in a commercial advertising the vehicle. In this case persuasion travels over the peripheral route and your attitude changes because you perceive the source of the communication to have some expertise.

The ELM suggests that both the central and peripheral routes can lead to attitude change. However, a key factor seems to be the degree to which a person actually thinks about the persuasive message. After all, the more you think about an idea, the more likely you are to remember it. Knowing this, which route to persuasion would you suspect to be more effective? Research indicates that persuasion via the central route leads to longer lasting attitude change. This is because people being persuaded via the central route are attending to and evaluating the evidence itself. When persuasion takes place via the peripheral route, those being persuaded are affected primarily by the emotions of the moment and are not paying much attention to whether the evidence is actually worthwhile. Because they think less about the issues, their attitudes are less likely to remain affected after the source departs.

You've probably seen many television commercials whose content has nothing at all to do with the quality of the product. Advertisers know that people are usually unmotivated to pay much attention to commercials so a detailed description of a product's superiority will often fall on deaf ears. They therefore often use the peripheral route by employing celebrities and other attractive people to appear on screen along with the product being advertised. If an advertiser can manage to grab viewers' attention and motivate them to pay attention to the message, central route persuasion will be more effective in changing people's attitudes. Because this is very difficult to do, advertisers use the peripheral route by capitalizing on the attractiveness and emotional evocativeness of the source.

CHANGING OUR OWN ATTITUDES

Sometimes others persuade us to change our attitudes. At other times, however, our attitudes are changed by our own thoughts and actions. Cognitive dissonance theory and self-perception theory both help us understand how this occurs. Although they propose different psychological processes, both illustrate how we are sometimes our own persuaders.

Cognitive Dissonance

The theory of **cognitive dissonance** was proposed in the 1950s by social psychologist Leon Festinger. Festinger wanted to understand what happens when a person simultaneously holds two thoughts that are contradictory. He predicted that when a person's thoughts—or thoughts and behavior—are inconsistent, that person will experience a feeling of dissonance or psychological tension. Festinger expected that the person's motivation to eliminate this tension would lead to attitude shifts that reduce the conflict. For example, if you are like most people, you are aware that smoking is extremely harmful to one's health. The research and media coverage have been so widespread for so many years that it would be difficult to be unaware of this fact. However, imagine you are a smoker. There could be many reasons for this behavior, but the behavior is clearly in conflict with your belief that smoking is unhealthy. This conflict between your thoughts and your behavior would cause you to experience uncomfortable tension that you would then be motivated to eliminate. You could eliminate the tension by not smoking. This would bring your behavior in line with your attitudes so there would be no more conflict. However, many times people respond to this type of conflict by bringing their attitudes in line with their behavior. Instead of quitting smoking, you might convince yourself that the research on smoking is flawed. Although certainly less wise that quitting, this attitude shift would also reduce your cognitive dissonance.

In 1959, in a now famous study, Festinger and his colleague James Carlsmith conducted the first formal test of dissonance theory. The study involved observing what happens when people act in ways that are inconsistent with their true attitudes. Festinger recruited college students for an ambiguous sounding experiment. In the experiment, participants spent an entire hour performing the very tedious tasks of placing and removing spools from a wooden tray and turning pegs in a pegboard. There was no challenge or puzzle to solve, so performing these tasks for such an extended period was guaranteed to be extraordinarily boring. After the hour had passed and the study was supposedly over, the experimenter asked the participant to tell the next participant who was waiting outside that the task was enjoyable, interesting, and exciting. In other words, the researchers asked the participants to express an opinion that was clearly at odds with their true attitude. Until this point in the study all participants were treated the same. However, in exchange for deliberately passing along false information to the next participant in line, half of the participants were given one dollar and half were given twenty dollars. Later all of the participants were asked about how much they enjoyed the experiment.

Having read the description of Festinger's experiment, who would you predict would later remember the experimental tasks as more interesting—those who received one dollar or those who received twenty dollars? Keeping in mind that this study was conducted more than 50 years ago when twenty dollars was a more significant sum of money than it might be today and also keeping in mind that the tasks were designed specifically to be extremely boring and tedious, many people would expect that those getting twenty dollars would have reported a higher level of enjoyment and interest. After all, they received more money. Festinger, however, correctly predicted that those who received only one dollar would recall the experiment more positively. And indeed, participants who received only one dollar not only rated the experiment as more enjoyable, but also expressed greater desire to participate in a similar experiment.

So why did this occur? The answer is cognitive dissonance. Those who received greater compensation for expressing a view that contradicted their true opinion experienced little dissonance. The pressure from their environment (i.e., the twenty dollars) provided a good reason for expressing an opinion that contradicted their true attitude, but they remained aware that what they expressed was not what they believed. Thus, when they were later asked about the study, their true attitude remained stable and in place. In contrast, those receiving one dollar as compensation had a much weaker reason for behaving inconsistently with their attitudes. They therefore experienced greater psychological tension from the contradiction, and they reduced this tension by shifting their attitude. Once they expressed the contradictory view of the study tasks (i.e., the tedious act of moving of spools and pegs around), their attitude fell in line with their behavior (i.e., telling someone else the task was interesting) and they remembered the tasks more positively to justify their actions.

At this point you might recognize that cognitive dissonance is often the reason that people rationalize their behaviors—meaning they do something and later look for ways to justify what they did. People who would swear that stealing is wrong take office supplies from work and convince themselves that it's not stealing; people who state that generosity is important but fail to donate money to charities or otherwise help their communities, convince themselves that such acts are not important. The alternative to this change in attitude is uncomfortable dissonance.

No Dissonance Required? Self-Perception Theory

A few years after Leon Festinger published his theory of cognitive dissonance, a researcher named Daryl Bem offered a different explanation for the attitude change observed in dissonance studies. Bem pointed out that most dissonance studies did not assess whether participants actually experienced any psychological tension. Rather dissonance researchers created conditions where participants' attitudes and behavior were inconsistent, observed the attitude change that occurred, and *inferred* that the attitude change was the result of tension. Bem was critical of researchers who explained human behavior based on unseen and unmeasured psychological states.

Bem then proposed his **self-perception theory** as an alternative to dissonance theory. Interestingly, self-perception theory and dissonance theory generally make the same predictions about attitude change, but they propose different explanations for the change. Bem sought a more straightforward explanation that did not require researchers to make assumptions about a psychological state of tension that was difficult to observe. He argued that in many cases, tension is not necessary for attitude change to occur. Instead, he suggested that we simply observe our own behavior and draw conclusions in much the same way that others would when observing our behavior. If you stay at a job even though you earn little money, a friend might infer that you like your job. In fact, you yourself might infer from your own behavior that you like the job. Both of you make the same observation and arrive at the same conclusion even though your friend would not experience dissonance about the issue. Bem therefore concluded that in such cases we need not make guesses about unseen psychological processes. Instead, he proposed, we can understand attitude development and change as resulting from normal observational and learning processes.

Self-perception theory offered an intriguing alternative to cognitive dissonance theory and provided a simpler explanation of apparent contradictions because it required less guesswork about people's motivations. Later research offered support for both theories but indicated that they probably operate at different times. The mechanisms proposed by self-perception theory seem to be at work when a person's attitude about something is not well-defined. For example, if you thought to yourself, "I never watch romantic movies so I guess I really don't like them," you would be engaging in self-perception. Because you did not have a strong attitude prior to recognizing your behavior, you simply inferred your attitude from things you have already done. When attitudes are already well-defined and firmly established, change is more likely to result from dissonance. If you strongly dislike romantic movies but you watch one with your friends and enjoy it, the dissonance might either weaken your attitude about romantic movies or lead you to remember the movie as less enjoyable. Either option would serve to reduce the inconsistency between your thoughts thereby reducing the tension.

There are many situations in everyday life in which the effects of self-perception and cognitive dissonance can be observed. Imagine that you are shopping for a car. After much research you have narrowed your choice to two models. The first has a sunroof and a better stereo; the second costs less and gets better gas mileage. You struggle with the decision for days or weeks because you just can't seem to decide which car is the better option. They seem equivalent in their overall value to you. However, when you finally decide on one model and sign the paperwork for your purchase, an interesting thing happens. Almost immediately you feel much more strongly that the car you purchased was the right one. This occurs regardless of which one you chose. If you chose the first car, you might suddenly see greater value in having a sunroof and a great stereo while minimizing the importance of gas mileage and cost. If you chose the second car, you might suddenly realize that the stereo and sunroof were impractical for you and that you're better off with good gas mileage and a smaller car payment.

Such changes in attitude often occur as a result of behavior. Once we make a decision—especially an irreversible one—our brains kick in and help us to convince ourselves that we made the right choice. Whether we attribute this to self-perception ("I bought this car so I must really like it and I must not have liked the other car as much") or cognitive dissonance ("I'm feeling tension because fuel economy is important but I bought a car with bad gas mileage— well, I guess gas mileage really isn't that important), the end result is that our attitudes change. So if you've done your research and you're still having trouble deciding which car (or anything else) to buy don't worry—once you've made the purchase, dissonance and self-perception will take over and whatever decision you made will feel like it was the correct one.

SUMMARY

Attitudes and attitude changes are inherently complex, and research results on these topics often yield unanticipated results. We acquire attitudes in a variety of ways, and people use many different persuasive techniques to shift our attitudes in one direction or another. Attitudes are often effective for predicting a person's behavior in the long run but may offer less insight into the same person's behavior in any single situation. Cognitive dissonance and self-perception theories explain how, in some cases, we act first and then make inferences about our attitudes from observing our own behavior. As you may have guessed after reading this chapter, research has revealed many nuances to attitude and persuasion processes. As with many areas of psychology, the answer to questions about the influence of attitudes or the most effective method of persuasion is often "it depends." You can get a better idea of the details by exploring the resources listed at the end of this chapter.

Further Reading

Ajzen, Icek, and Martin Fishbein. The Influence of Attitudes on Behavior. In *The Handbook of Attitudes*, eds. Dolores Albarracín, Blair T. Johnson, and Mark P. Zanna, 173–221. Mahwah, N.J.: Lawrence Erlbaum Associates Publishers, 2005.

Bohner, Gerd, and Norbert Schwarz. Attitudes, Persuasion, & Behavior. In *Blackwell Handbook of Social Psychology: Intraindividual Processes*, eds. Abraham Tesser and Norbert Schwarz, 413–435. Malden, Mass.: Wiley-Blackwell, 2003.

Festinger, Leon. *A Theory of Cognitive Dissonance.* Stanford University Press, 1962.

CHAPTER 3

CONFORMITY, COMPLIANCE, AND OBEDIENCE

The presence of others can have a profound impact on our behavior. Sometimes we are aware of the influence of others and sometimes not. In some cases there is real social pressure to act in a particular way, and in other cases the pressure exists primarily in our own minds, but our behavior changes just the same. This section explains how some of the most powerful social pressures exert their effects. It will also explain how and why we might change our opinions and attitudes as a result of pressure from others, although we more frequently change only our behavior and continue to maintain views—even while those views remain concealed from others. A simple example readily illustrates this concept: Your boss tells you to wash the windows, and you think doing this is a waste of time. You will probably obey his or her instructions but may still see the task as a waste of time, even after you've completed it.

Whether we are conforming, complying, or obeying, the result is a change in behavior, regardless of how we think or feel about the behavior. In fact, it is very common for social pressures to cause us to behave in ways that are inconsistent with our true desires or interests. You might, for example, purchase a particular shirt even though you dislike the color because your friends wear the same brand (conformity). You might agree to pay an acquisition fee on a new car even though it means a higher total price than the salesperson originally offered, mostly because it's easier to do this than to haggle (compliance). And you might do your homework or sweep the floor because your teachers or parents tell you to, even though there is something you would much rather be doing (obedience).

One thing that distinguishes conformity, compliance, and obedience lies in the degree to which the social pressure you experience is explicit or subtle. Another is the presence or absence of a power differential between you and the people exerting the pressure.

CONFORMITY

Conformity refers to our tendency to act in ways that are consistent with what those around us are doing. The pressure to conform can be remarkably powerful. The concept works in much the same way as peer pressure. We often change our behavior to fit in with valued people around us. Although some people conform more than others and everyone conforms more in some situations than in others, most of us know that it can feel quite uncomfortable to be out of sync with others. This is especially true when those around us are people with whom we strongly identify and whose friendship or respect we value. Many times conformity pressures are real and there is little question about what is acceptable behavior in a particular situation. Other times the pressure to conform is less explicit and can even be something we imagine. When everyone around us dresses in a particular way, we often feel that we should do the same in order to fit in. We feel that others might be evaluating us and that failure to comply might hurt our chances of getting a date, getting a loan, or getting a job. Certainly it is wise to look one's best in many situations, but there are also situations where we conform to the behavior of those around us without ever knowing whether anyone is really paying any attention at all.

Picture yourself arriving for a college class. You arrive a few minutes before the class is scheduled to start and see a large group of students waiting outside the lecture hall. You also notice that the doors to the lecture hall are closed. You decide that the previous class must still be in session, so the students in your class are waiting until the students in the previous class leave. You are tempted to look inside the room, but surely someone checked before you arrived to make sure that the room was in use. What you are not aware of is that the first few people to arrive failed to check the room and that every subsequent student assumed just what you have. Each new arrival encounters a larger group of waiting students and is therefore even more certain that the room is in use. Even if you decide to check for yourself, you will likely feel a bit strange as you move past many people to open the classroom doors. Everyone present is conforming. If you open that door, you are bucking the behavioral trend of every other person in the group. What are the chances you would do so?

One of the first researchers to study conformity in a systematic way was Solomon Asch. Beginning in the 1940s and continuing for many years, Asch investigated the factors that influence our likelihood of following the crowd versus acting independently. Asch developed a simple but ingenious method for testing (in a laboratory) the limits of conformity. He recruited college students to participate in a study of visual perception. As each subject arrived for the study, he or she entered a room where several other participants were waiting. The experimenter soon revealed a simple visual perception task. Participants saw an image of a target line and three other lines to which the target was to be compared. The participants were instructed to identify from the three lines the one that was the same length as the target line. The task was constructed so that the correct answer would be obvious to anyone with reasonable eyesight. Had the participants responded privately, they would have easily indicated the correct line. What the participant did not know, however, was that the other students in the room were partners in the experiment and had been directed in advance to provide a consistent but incorrect answer. Asch wanted to know whether people would provide an answer that their senses told them was clearly incorrect, simply because others had provided that answer.

Asch's findings illustrate the amazing power of conformity pressures. Upon repeated trials, three-quarters of his participants conformed at least once, providing an answer that was obviously incorrect after hearing others do so. Furthermore, one out of three participants conformed at least half of the time, with

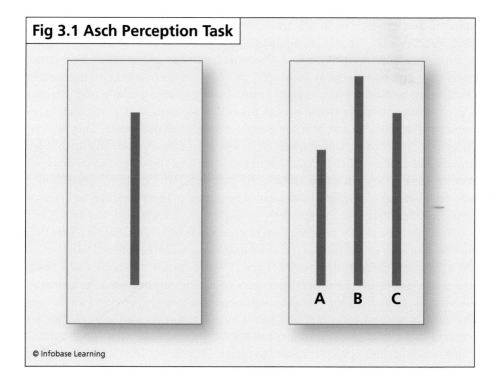

Fig 3.1 Asch Perception Task

A   B   C

© Infobase Learning

some conforming nearly every time. These results show that when people must choose between an action dictated by immediate group pressures and one dictated by their own clear perceptions of reality, they often choose to follow the crowd even when the crowd is quite wrong.

You may have noticed from the results described in the paragraph above that not everyone conformed to subtle group pressure. If three-quarters of the people conformed at least once, it must be recognized that one in four of Asch's initial participants never conformed. Asch attributed this to individual characteristics such as personality traits.

As Asch's work progressed, he discovered a number of other factors that affect the likelihood of conformity. One thing he noted was that a number of situational factors can increase or decrease conformity. He observed for example that for conformity pressures to be at their peak, a group must be unanimous in its judgment. In the context of Asch's visual perception task described above, this would mean that every person in the group would have given the same incorrect answer. If even one person (other than the actual participant) gave the correct answer, the likelihood of conformity decreased dramatically. You may have experienced this phenomenon among groups of friends deciding on a recreational activity. When it seems that everyone is in agreement about what to do but you would like to do something different, you are far more likely to speak your mind if you know that at least one other person agrees with your opinion. You may still be in the minority within the group, but feeling that you have someone on your side is empowering.

Another important variable Asch considered was group size. Conducting trials with groups as large as 16 people, he observed no meaningful increase in conformity beyond a group size of three. In other words, conformity reaches a peak when just three other people unanimously express a particular viewpoint so that the addition of more people makes little difference. This is especially important to consider when we try to understand peer pressure. If we understand that pressure to conform to the actions of those around us does not require large groups in order to be quite powerful, we can easily grasp how a very small group of people who appear to be united in their view can be extraordinarily influential.

Perhaps the most interesting thing to keep in mind about Asch's research is that no one told any of the participants to give an incorrect answer. As is often the case when conformity pressures are at work, no direct orders were given, and participants faced no overt pressure to act or respond in a certain way. So what happened? When the others present consistently provided a response that clearly seemed incorrect, it likely caused confusion and uncertainty for the real subjects of the research. This uncertainty probably led some participants to doubt their perceptions and to retreat into the comfort and certainty of being part of the majority. The same processes are often at work in everyday life.

The Bright Side of Conformity

After reading about conformity research it is easy to think of the tendency to act like those around us as a bad thing. In some cultures, including in the predominant culture in the United States, people prefer to think of themselves as individuals who are able to assert their distinct identities without being controlled by the actions of others. It is certainly true that we are often able to overcome conformity pressures and to behave as individuals. At the same time, it is equally true that the tendency to conform is not a flaw in human character. Conformity allows us to establish and maintain stable social groups and to develop a sense of affiliation with those around us. Like most human behaviors, the tendency to conform can be beneficial; it becomes harmful when it is carried to extremes.

Sometimes we change our behavior because others have talked us into doing something, but often all it takes is a belief that everyone around us is doing or thinking the same thing.

COMPLIANCE

When the pressure to act moves beyond subtle cues based on majority opinion and we are quite certain of what someone expects of us, we have moved beyond conformity and entered the realm of compliance. Unlike conformity, where the pressure to behave in a particular way may be only in one's head, **compliance** involves far more specific social pressure to do specific things. When we are aware of these pressures, we have little doubt that they are real and we are usually quite certain of what we are expected to do. As is true when we obey directions to do something, compliance involves changing behavior to fit the wishes of someone else. The key difference, however, is that the person attempting to influence us to comply with some desired behavior does not necessarily have any real authority over us. Compliance techniques are therefore quite useful for those who wish to convince us to engage in some behavior but who do not have any real recourse if we do not do what they wish. Compliance techniques are effective because they capitalize on the way people normally think and on people's sense of fair play.

Many people who wish to gain compliance from others attempt to activate a social norm known as the **norm of reciprocity**. This is the principle of give and take that that guides many of our social interactions. In simple terms, it means that we should help others who help us. If your friend who was absent from class asks to borrow your notes in order to catch up, you will likely expect him or her to return the favor when you miss a class. If the favor is denied after you granted a similar favor, you are likely to feel a sense of injustice, and you may even feel betrayed. For another example, imagine attending a holiday party and receiving a gift from a friend or family member for whom you failed to bring a gift. The discomfort you feel at that moment arises because the norm of reciprocity has been activated but you have failed to comply with it. Interestingly, we often feel uncomfortable in this situation even if people agreed in advance to bring no gifts. The norm of reciprocity is so powerful that we feel guilt even when we did exactly what was agreed upon.

The norm of reciprocity certainly serves an important function in social interaction. If people felt no obligation to return favors or treat others as well as they have been treated, a great many interpersonal and societal problems would result. However, our tendency to return favors can also be used deliberately by those wishing to change our behavior. Perhaps nowhere is this more evident than in the case of charitable agencies seeking donations. For example, you or people you know have probably received address labels in the mail from charitable organizations. The labels are printed with your address, often with pleasant pictures or drawings on them as well. Along with the labels is a letter emphasizing that the labels are free but also describing how desperately the organization needs money. The agency sending these labels is using the norm of reciprocity to increase the likelihood that you will donate money. The objective is for you to perceive the labels as a gift and then feel an obligation to give something in return. Although most people who receive the labels do not send money, the charity sends the labels to thousands of people so only a small number need to comply for the effort to be successful. As is the case when we fail to bring a gift and then receive one, we may feel slight pangs of guilt if we use the labels without making a contribution. It is very important to note that many charities help large numbers of people and are in desperate need of funding. A charity's use of the norm of reciprocity should not in itself be a reason to dislike the organization. Many charities must do whatever they can to raise money, and they use this strategy because it works. Our awareness of the strategy is important but need not prevent us from recognizing the importance of the cause.

Use of the norm of reciprocity to increase compliance is not limited to charities. You have most likely encountered many other situations where the norm was being deliberately activated. For instance, when you are stopped at a traffic light and someone approaches your car and washes the windshield; when you visit a museum where admission is free but there is a donation box inside the door; when a retail store offers a free gift just for coming in; and when stores offer free samples of products or free makeovers. The words "no obligation" mean that you are not making a formal agreement to buy anything; they do not, however, guarantee that there will be no social obligation to do something.

A second example of a compliance technique that can be remarkably effective despite the user's lack of any genuine power or authority is known as the **foot-in-the-door technique**. This technique gets its name from the time when it was common for businesses to dispatch door-to-door salesmen to sell their products. The idea was that once a salesman got his foot in the door, the prospective customer would be unable to shut him out. In a broader sense, the technique involves making a small request that is likely to be accommodated and then following up with a bigger request. You may have had the experience of walking through a mall and being approached by someone holding a clipboard who asks for "just a moment of your time." After you agree and sit down to answer a few questions for a survey, the surveyor might ask whether you would be willing to participate in a more lengthy survey or watch a sales video about a product. Agreeing to answer a few questions requiring just a brief time commitment on your part, leaves you open to a setup for a more significant commitment. The foot-in-the-door technique capitalizes on our reluctance to reverse course after making a commitment, even if the commitment itself changes. In the mall example, you suddenly find yourself facing a new decision—whether to stay and comply to an additional parameter of the original request or to reverse your prior willingness to help by walking away. Anyone who has experienced this compliance technique knows how difficult it is to walk away.

In an early and interesting test of the foot-in-the-door technique, researchers Jonathan Freedman and Scott Fraser conducted an experiment by randomly contacting people from a telephone directory. Imagine you receive a telephone call from a man who tells you he is from a consumers' association and he would like to send a team of approximately five men to your home for two hours to inventory your household products. The man also tells you that the team of investigators must have access to all storage areas of your home. Would you agree to his request and allow the team to visit your home?

If you are like most people, you are probably scratching your head in disbelief at the absurdity of this question. Surely almost everyone would object to having a team of unknown men enter their homes to search the storage areas. And you would be correct in this assumption—provided that the only background information you have is that people received this call and nothing else. Indeed, only a few people in Freedman and Fraser's study agreed to this request; the vast majority did not. The twist here is that some people who were contacted for the study encountered a different scenario. Like the first group, they received a call requesting that a team of investigators be granted access to their homes. However, these individuals had received a call from the same person three days earlier. During this initial call, they were asked to participate in a brief telephone survey about household products. Among the people who had received this earlier call and who had agreed to participate in the brief telephone survey, more than half agreed to the home visit from the investigators. That is, those initially presented only with the large and unreasonable request tended not to comply. Those who received a smaller and more reasonable request in advance were far more likely to comply with the bigger request that came later.

Why is the foot-in-the-door technique an effective way of gaining compliance? One reason is our tendency to behave consistently. Most of us find it difficult to change direction once we have committed to a course of action. Although the stakes may get higher and the costs we incur more extreme, the desire we feel to walk away is overrun by the pressure we feel to remain consistent. This is especially true when we help others. Once we agree to a request, we feel obligated to continue agreeing even when the costs increase. Once you agree to help someone by contributing to a charity or answering some questions on a survey, you no longer have the excuse that you never do those kinds of things. In many cases, you can't come up with a different excuse. Self-image also plays a role in our vulnerability to the foot-in-the-door technique. Helping in the first place reminds us that we want to be helpful to people in general. Refusing to help would then be even more difficult because it would conflict with our activated identity as helpful people. Although we may sometimes be aware that the foot-in-the-door strategy is being used to affect our behavior, this often fails to eliminate the pressure we feel to keep our behavior consistent. Changing course is almost always psychologically difficult.

A third technique used to gain compliance is often thought of as the reverse of the foot-in-the-door technique. Known as the **door-in-the-face technique,** it involves making an initial large request that is almost certain to be denied. The name of this strategy comes from the idea that when you make such a large and unreasonable request, the person you are speaking to is likely to slam the door in your face. Once your initial large request has been denied, you can then make a smaller and more reasonable request that reflects what you were actually seeking in the first place. You have made your true request seem far more reasonable by creating a comparison with one that was unrealistic.

One of the first formal tests of the door-in-the-face technique was conducted by Robert Cialdini and his colleagues. Cialdini predicted that a person making only a small request of another person would be less likely to gain compliance than a person who makes a large request prior to the small request. In this study, a college student individually approached other students on a university campus and asked them to volunteer to supervise a group of delinquent youths during a visit to a zoo. The zoo trip was to last two hours, and the volunteers would not be paid for their time. All the students who were approached were asked this question, but half were first asked to serve as unpaid counselors at a juvenile detention facility for two hours per week for two years. Very few of the students who were asked only to assist with the zoo trip agreed to help. However among those who first heard and denied the request to serve as counselors for two years, half agreed to help with the zoo trip. The contrast with the initial unreasonable request greatly increased the likelihood that people would comply with the smaller request. Follow-up studies by Cialdini and his colleagues showed that the door-in-the-face technique can increase the likelihood of obtaining compliance even on rather significant requests—as long as the initial request is greater and more unreasonable than the actual desired request.

There are a couple of likely reasons that the door-in-the-face technique is effective for gaining compliance. As mentioned above, the contrast between the initial large request and the smaller request makes the actual request seem far more reasonable by comparison. Moreover, many people find it difficult to turn down two consecutive requests—especially when both requests involve helping others (as was the case in Cialdini's research). However, the door-in-the-face strategy is also effective for gaining compliance with requests that do not involve helping others. There must therefore be other psychological factors at work. The most likely of these involves a dimension of the norm of reciprocity (discussed above). This norm is the basis of compromise in social interaction. Recall that the norm of reciprocity dictates that if we receive a gift, favor, or concession from someone, we are obligated to return that favor when possible. In the case of the door-in-the-face approach a person first asks us for a large favor which we deny. We are likely to perceive the person's shift to a smaller request as a concession, and this activates our awareness of the norm of reciprocity. When this happens we feel a social obligation to compromise and the only way to do so is to grant the smaller request. Like any compliance technique this approach is not foolproof, but its application greatly increases the likelihood that a request will be granted.

There are many ways that the door-in-the-face strategy is used in everyday life. Imagine a teenager asking his parents for $100 for a new pair of jeans. Many parents would consider this unreasonable and would quickly deny the request. When the request for $100 is turned down, the teen then asks for $10 to see a movie. In light of the initial large figure, the request for $10 seems quite modest. Another example would be a young child asking his mother for a large piece of cake before dinner. When this request is denied, the child asks for a cookie instead. Although the child actually wanted the cookie, asking for the cake first increased the chance that the smaller request would be granted.

One of the most common areas of life where compliance techniques can be observed is in the world of product sales. A salesperson's livelihood requires obtaining compliance from others, even though he or she has no power over those others. Salespeople spend much of their lives in situations where they must use subtle strategies to affect others' behavior. Although effective salespeople use a variety of social psychological techniques (including those you've already read about), to increase their sales volume, there is one compliance technique that is most consistent with the salesperson stereotype. This technique is known as low balling and occurs when two people arrive at an agreement about something. After the agreement is made, one of the parties then attempts to change the terms of the agreement in his or her own favor, thus increasing the other person's cost.

One example of the **low-ball technique** occurs when a customer visits a car dealership and agrees to purchase a car at a particular price. Even after the agreement has been made, there are a number of ways that the salesperson may try to inflate the agreed-upon cost. For example, when the customer sits down to complete the paperwork for the transaction, the invoice may contain previously undisclosed costs, such as dealer and acquisition fees, as well as fees for cleaning or rust proofing the vehicle. Although these fees increase the total cost to the customer, many people proceed with the purchase despite the change(s) in the agreement. Many of us probably believe we would be immune to this technique and would walk away from the deal. This is certainly true for some people in some situations, but the technique is often used and often effective so there must be a reason that it works.

Robert Cialdini and his colleagues, who have conducted research on a variety of compliance techniques, offer some insight into the psychological processes that are functioning when we encounter the low-ball strategy. One explanation for the effectiveness of low-balling is that once we proceed with a particular action (such as making a purchase), simple psychological inertia makes it unlikely that we will change course. It is usually easier to proceed with an action than to reverse it. This is especially true with decisions of significant magnitude, such as purchasing a car. A vehicle is the second most expensive purchase that most people ever make (next to purchasing a home). This increases the level of emotion involved in the decision, which can cause people to ignore or minimize glitches such as a relatively small increase in price. Once a person passes the difficult hurdle of deciding, he or she may prefer to pay a little extra to avoid having to go through the process again at a different dealership. In addition, most people do a fair amount of research about various vehicle models before they decide which one to purchase. Several models may seem very similar before a decision is made, but once a person decides to purchase a specific model he or she will tend to rationalize the decision by recalling the positive characteristics of the chosen vehicle and the negative characteristics of the cars that were not purchased. This would also make a person less likely to walk away rather than pay the extra money for the selected vehicle.

We should keep in mind that many salespeople are very honest and do not use deliberately coercive strategies to manipulate their customers. However you can now understand that many people—ourselves included—use well-established social psychological techniques to alter other people's behavior. Perhaps the most impressive characteristic of compliance techniques is that they are so effective despite the fact that the user has no genuine authority. Compliance strategies cause changes in our behavior—even if our private attitudes and opinions remain constant. If our behavior is subject to the influence of those who

Cults

Many people wonder how cult leaders are able to exercise dominance over seemingly normal people and to manipulate their followers' behavior even to the point of murder and suicide. In fact, the techniques that cult leaders use to recruit followers and manipulate behavior are well known in the psychological literature. Cult leaders tend to target as recruits people who are young and people who are in psychological distress. When people are anxious or fearful, they tend to seek out affiliation with others and the cult offers opportunities for supportive social interaction. Once a person becomes part of the group, he or she is cut off from prior relationships and lives in a restricted environment where prior beliefs and values are systematically dismantled. The unanimity of the group's views makes it difficult to recognize alternative options, and soon the conformity, compliance, and even obedience pressures imposed by the group cause the person to act in ways that are at odds with his or her prior identity. Finally cognitive dissonance, which you read about in Chapter 2, leads the person to justify these behaviors and a new identity begins to emerge. This is a simplified description of the process, but the techniques that allow cult leaders to dominate others are anything but mysterious.

have no power over us, imagine how much more our behavior might change when someone does have authority. This is the case in situations that demand obedience.

OBEDIENCE

Imagine you are driving down a street in your hometown on a route that you frequently travel. You encounter a police officer directing traffic who points you toward a route that you never use. Do you follow the officer's instructions or do you simply pass by and ignore his authority? In such a situation, nearly all of us do what we are told. When our parents, teachers, bosses, or other authority figures instruct us to do something, we usually obey with very little thought. This is the case even when the perceived authority has little actual power to punish us if we disobey. Generally our tendency to obey authority figures is a good thing. Imagine a society where every citizen suddenly began ignoring parents, teachers, police, government agents, etc., in favor of personal interests and preferences. Such a society would very quickly dissolve into utter chaos. **Obedience** serves a purpose. However, imagine that a person in authority orders you to do something that could be harmful to someone else. Would you obey? Most people think they would resist the person's authority and act according to their own conscience. However, research initiated in the 1960s and replicated time and again since then suggests that in this respect, what many people think they know about themselves is inaccurate.

In the early 1960s, a researcher at Yale University named Stanley Milgram began what would become one of the most famous psychological studies ever done. To understand the context that inspired Milgram's work, readers should note that at this point in history many former leaders from Nazi Germany were being brought to trial for war crimes committed during World War II. During the war, millions of European citizens (mostly Jews) were rounded up on orders from Nazi officials and sent to concentration camps where more than 6 million ultimately died. After the war, the atrocities committed by the Nazis were exposed in great detail and many of the officers and guards responsible were apprehended and tried for their crimes.

Milgram's research was inspired less by the events themselves than in the explanations that nearly all of the accused war criminals offered in their own defense. Claiming that they had sympathized with their victims, the defendants argued that they had no choice. They insisted that they were simply following orders and doing their jobs. It was a defense that many people listened to with understandable doubt.

Responding to the Nazi defendants' claims, Milgram designed a complex scenario in which research volunteers would be directed by an authority figure to administer electric shocks to another person. Milgram's research program was a detailed examination of just how far people would go when instructed by a person in authority to harm another individual. What he found was both profoundly surprising and profoundly disturbing.

Imagine yourself in the following situation: You volunteer to participate in a psychological study about teaching and learning. Upon arrival at the laboratory, you are introduced to another participant and a random drawing puts you in the role of the teacher and your co-participant in the role of the learner. Next you watch as the learner is strapped into a chair and connected to electrodes through which you will administer shocks if he does not perform successfully on a memory task. During this process you also hear the learner mention to the experimenter—the authority figure wearing a white lab coat—that he has a mild heart condition.

After the learner is strapped in and given instructions, you follow the experimenter to an adjacent room where you are instructed to sit in front of a shock generator that you will use to punish the learner when he responds incorrectly. The generator has a long line of switches that are labeled both with the number of volts that each will deliver, and with verbal descriptors indicating the severity of the shock. The switches range from 15 volts on the far left to 450 volts on the far right. The verbal descriptors range from "mild shock" to "danger severe shock" and the 450-volt switch is labeled simply with three black Xs. The experimenter tells you how to conduct the memory test and you are told that with each incorrect answer from the learner, you must administer the next most severe shock. As the session progresses and you administer increasingly severe shocks, you hear increasingly dramatic screams of pain from the learner. He screams that he cannot stand the pain and he demands to be released. Eventually he falls silent and gives no response either to the test questions or to repeated severe shocks. Throughout the process, the researcher calmly and authoritatively insists that you must go on with the experiment.

There are several important things you should know to better understand Milgram's study, things none of the participants were told beforehand. The learner was a partner in the research rather than a participant in the study, and it was the behavior of the participants, not the learner, that was actually being observed and measured. Most importantly, no shocks of any kind were given to the learner. This was not a study of learning or punishment. It was a study of obedience.

Without knowing these important facts, would you continue to administer shocks after the learner screamed to be let out? Would you continue inflicting severe pain on another person because someone in authority told you to do so? Like most people, you would be shocked at these questions and emphatically insist that you would not continue. And you would also be very surprised that one of the interesting aspects of Milgram's study was his conclusion that people are often astoundingly certain but also incorrect about how they would respond to a situation that they have not in fact experienced.

Nearly everyone, upon hearing of this scenario, would insist that they would not continue administering shocks and would resist the authority of the experimenter. In fact, psychiatrists predicted prior to the start of Milgram's study that only one in one thousand people would continue with the experiment long enough to administer the highest level of shock—450 volts. In fact, approximately two-thirds of the participants did administer this highest level shock. Although many of them showed very clear and dramatic distress at having to proceed, and even asked the researcher to check on the learner, most people eventually continued until the most severe shock had been administered. These results shocked everyone—including Milgram.

Perhaps at this point you are thinking to yourself that this level of obedience to an authority is a thing of the past. After all, these studies were conducted nearly a half century ago. Perhaps people today are more independent and would be less likely to obey orders that could harm another person. Unfortunately this does not appear to be the case.

From time to time stories appear in the news that demonstrate how difficult it is to disobey orders when we believe they came from a person with authority. One particularly horrific example occurred on April 9, 2004 when a man claiming to be a police office telephoned a McDonald's restaurant in Mount Washington, Kentucky. The caller informed a manager that one of the restaurant's employees was suspected of a theft and that the female employee should be taken to the restaurant's office and searched. Following the caller's instructions—which ultimately took more than three hours and involved several people including one manager's fiancé—the employee was stripped naked, forced to perform a variety of humiliating acts, and was eventually sexually assaulted.

Subsequent actions by other employees helped reveal the call to be a hoax. The call had come from hundreds of miles away and eventually the caller was apprehended. However, the caller was never convicted of any crime in connection with the incident whereas the male involved in the employee's interrogation pled guilty to several crimes and was sentenced to prison. All of this took place because someone on the telephone, claiming to have police authority, had ordered that the acts be performed. Although it is certainly not true that all people would follow harmful orders to this extreme, the process is not all that different from when a teacher tells us to complete an assignment, our parents tell us to take out the trash, or a police officer tells us to turn down our music because we are disturbing the neighbors. Like us, those at the restaurant were simply following orders because they did not believe they had a choice, a claim chillingly similar to the defense offered by the Nazi war criminals that inspired Milgram's study.

Remember that obedience is about behavior—not whether you like what you are doing or what you would do if you had a choice. Although Milgram's extensive research and subsequent obedience studies have taught us a great deal about human behavior and have revealed something about the darker sides of human nature, many have criticized such work on ethical grounds. In part because of the obvious mental anguish that research participants sometimes exhibited during obedience studies, all psychological research must now be approved by the sponsoring institution's (usually a college or university) human subjects review board. It is the job of these ethics boards to evaluate proposed research projects in advance to anticipate and prevent potential harm to participants. You may wonder why such procedures are necessary when participants do not face any risk of physical harm. To answer this question, consider how you would feel if you unexpectedly found yourself in a situation where you were told that you had no choice but to administer severe electric shocks to someone who continuously screamed in pain and begged for you to stop. Most researchers likely would behave ethically and morally even without formal review procedures. Today's ethics review boards certainly prevent some studies from being conducted or replicated. Because of this, participants in psychological studies can be confident that someone in authority has their interests at heart.

The Stanford Prison Experiment

Milgram's work inspired many other researchers to explore the influences of social pressures on behavior. In 1971, researcher Philip Zimbardo transformed the basement of the psychology building at Stanford University into a makeshift prison. He then recruited psychologically healthy young men to become inmates and staff at the prison. Volunteers for the study were assigned randomly to become either prisoners or guards, and initially there were no noteworthy differences between those assigned to each role. However, once prisoners and guards began wearing their uniforms and functioning in the mock prison setting, their behavior quickly began to reflect the roles to which they had been assigned. Many of the guards, possessing authority based only on chance assignment to a role, treated the prisoners cruelly and subjected them to incredibly demeaning tasks. Many of the prisoners became passive or lashed out with great hostility toward the guards. The reactions became so severe that Zimbardo chose to discontinue the study much earlier than planned, on the basis of ethical obligations to protect research participants. This now famous study was one of many that helped to illustrate how easily we may adopt roles and behave accordingly—even when it means treating others badly.

SUMMARY

This chapter illustrated how pressure from others can have a profound impact on our behavior. When we conform, we are adapting our behavior to what we believe the majority around us expects. In some cases the pressure is in only our heads but this does not make it any less powerful in affecting our behavior. Sometimes the pressure from others becomes more explicit, and there is no question about what we are expected to do. People use a variety of compliance techniques to elicit specific behaviors from others over whom they have no true power or authority. Finally, we generally do what people in authority tell us to do, even when we would prefer not to obey. The many studies of these phenomena of social interaction are interesting if for no other reason than that they teach us that we often know far less about ourselves than we think. Most of us think we know how we would respond in various situations and most of us believe we would be able to resist social pressure. Some of us may be correct, but most of us are not.

Further Reading

Asch, S.E. *Effects of Group Pressure Upon the Modification and Distortion of Judgments.* Oxford, England: Carnegie Press, 1951.

Cialdini, Robert B. *Influence: Science and Practice.* 4th ed. Boston, Mass.: Allyn and Bacon, 2001.

Milgram, Stanley. "Behavioral Study of Obedience." Journal of Abnormal and Social Psychology 67, no. 4 (Oct 1963): 371–378.

CHAPTER 4

STEREOTYPING, PREJUDICE, AND DISCRIMINATION

The terms stereotyping, prejudice, and discrimination have different definitions but the concepts they represent are so intertwined that it is difficult to consider them in isolation. Stereotyping generally refers to a cognitive (thinking) process that involves categorizing people into identifiable groups and establishing beliefs about people based on their membership in these groups. Prejudice refers to negative emotions associated with people who are members of the stereotyped groups. Interestingly, stereotypes sometimes involve positive beliefs about members of certain groups, but prejudice usually manifests itself as negative emotions. Finally, discrimination refers to biased behaviors toward members of certain groups. Although it is possible for stereotypes to arise without associated prejudice or discrimination, there is often a close connection among thoughts, feelings, and behaviors about members of various social groups.

STEREOTYPING

What is the typical librarian like? What characteristics come to mind when you think of an airline pilot? How about an airline flight attendant? What are men like? What are women like? Your thoughts about these types of people and countless others likely reflect at least some stereotypical expectations. **Stereotypes** are shared beliefs about people who are members of certain groups. Stereotypes are also generalizations that are frequently inconsistent with reality but often contain some truth. For example, when you think of a typical elementary school teacher, you probably picture a woman rather than a man.

This clearly reflects a stereotypical belief, but the belief is largely accurate—the vast majority of elementary school teachers are women. Stereotypes are mental shortcuts that help us feel that we understand the world. Some more accurately reflect reality than others, but they nearly always impose limitations on those whose behaviors or characteristics do not conform to a given stereotype.

Where Do Stereotypes Come From?

At the most basic level, stereotyping is a cognitive process that places people into categories. Activating stereotypes is similar to activating other types of mental **schemas**. Our schemas are simply part of our mental system for organizing information and making sense of the world. For example, most of us have a schema (a set of expectations) for a classroom. As we enter a classroom, our mental schema is activated and we expect that we will see such things as student desks, a blackboard, possibly a computer, and so on. These are related characteristics that our mental schema ties in with the broader category of "classroom."

Stereotypes represent a specific type of schema in which information is organized in our minds around some specific social category. Just as we have expectations for the characteristics of a classroom, we likewise have expectations for the characteristics of different kinds of people. Just as entering a classroom elicits a host of expectations for what we will encounter, contact with or thoughts about various groups also bring about expectations. Stereotyping is therefore rooted in normal mental processes that our brains use to help us sort through immense quantities of social information to improve our understanding of the world.

The process of categorizing is generally helpful and adaptive because it allows us to make sense of massive amounts of information efficiently. It is not something we usually engage in voluntarily or even consciously. It is simply a normal consequence when our brains—with their limited memory and processing ability—must make sense of a great deal of complex information. This explanation may make stereotyping sound rather benign and harmless, at least in intent. However, it is important to recognize that categorizing can make us feel that we accurately understand the world even when we do not. That is, a stereotype does not actually have to be accurate or true. As long as we believe it to be accurate or true, it allows us to feel that we have insight about some person or some group.

Given our tendency to divide the world into categories, a second factor that leads to stereotyping is our related tendency to separate people into ingroups and outgroups. Your **ingroup** is made up of people with whom you tend to identify. Your **outgroup** consists of people whose group identity is somehow different from your own. For example, if you identify politically as a Republican you are likely to see fellow Republicans as your ingroup and Democrats as your outgroup. If you are a woman you may see men as an outgroup. If you are a

Muslim you may see Christians an outgroup. It is important to recognize that all human beings have many group identities that can be more or less relevant at different times. Imagine someone who is a woman, a Muslim, and a Republican. She may tend to perceive a man who is a Muslim and a Republican as part of her ingroup when issues of religion or politics are relevant, but part of the outgroup when gender issues are at the forefront. What matters most when determining whether someone is slotted into our respective ingroups or outgroups is which of our identities is most active at a particular point in time.

Research on perceptions of ingroups and outgroups has revealed that once our group identity is activated we tend to perceive members of the outgroup as much more similar to each other than they actually are. In other words, we see all of them as being the same. This is known as the **outgroup homogeneity effect**, and its impact is observable when we note distinctions between members of our own group (thus suggesting that our group has flexibility and is capable of nuance) but tend to overlook similar distinctions within other groups. In many cases this pattern results from the simple fact that we have more contact with members of our ingroup than with members of outgroups. More frequent interaction with a variety of people from our own group leads us to perceive that there is more variety within our group in general. In contrast, our contact with outgroup members is too limited to provide us with broad knowledge of that group, so our knowledge remains general and thus stereotypic. One outcome of stereotyping is that we come to appreciate differences among those who share some aspect of our own identity and can therefore appreciate that broad generalizations may not always be accurate. In contrast, our lack of similar experience with outgroup members leads us to perceive them as all the same so stereotypes are more likely to be viewed as accurate.

How Are Stereotypes Maintained?

Once a stereotype has been established in our minds, a host of well-researched psychological processes serve to strengthen it and convince us of its accuracy. For example, **illusory correlations** maintain and strengthen stereotypes. To understand this concept, it is important to recognize that a correlation is simply an association between two things. We can posit, for instance, that the number of hours that students spend studying is associated with how well they perform on exams. In this particular case, a correlation exists because there is an actual relationship between time spent studying and exam scores. Illusory correlations differ in that there *seems* to be an association between two things but our perception of such a relationship is flawed– the association is an illusion.

A good example of an illusory correlation is the relationship between politics and corruption. Many people hold the stereotype that politicians are dishonest, and a number of factors can contribute to our perception that politicians are more dishonest than other people. One of these factors is news reports about corrupt political dealings. These are quite commonplace, and many of us have come to expect that stories about politics will nearly always involve reports of dishonest behavior. But although there are certainly dishonest politicians, the real question is whether politicians as a group tend to be any more dishonest than people who are not politicians. The great number of news reports on the dishonest behavior of some politicians does not prove that all politicians or even most politicians are dishonest or corrupt, so this is may be an illusory correlation.

What specific factors might make this an illusory correlation? For one thing, illusory correlations can emerge when relatively uncommon behaviors, manifested by only a minority of members in a group, are generalized to all members of that group. It is likely that among both politicians and nonpoliticians, honest behaviors outnumber dishonest behaviors. That is most people—politicians or not—behave honestly most of the time so dishonest behaviors are less common than honest ones. It is in fact entirely possible that the proportion of dishonest politicians and the proportion of dishonest nonpoliticians is more or less the same. One key difference is that politicians are a minority group—most people are not politicians. Another difference is that media attention is more likely to focus on corrupt or dishonest behavior in this minority group rather than on similar behaviors in society at large. When relatively infrequent behaviors are observed and noted in people we notice because they are somehow different from the majority, we soon tend to perceive that the behaviors themselves are more common within that minority group. Thus the combination of distinctive behaviors and distinctive people promotes the establishment of illusory correlations.

A second factor that plays a role in generation of illusory correlations is known as **confirmation bias**—the tendency to see what we expect to see. This bias contributes greatly to our beliefs that certain behaviors and characteristics are more common among some groups. Once we have an established belief that politicians are dishonest, we will have a strong tendency to notice and remember things that confirm the stereotype. Conversely, we tend to minimize or may even fail to notice things that contradict the same stereotype. This process does not occur consciously or deliberately. It occurs because we are bombarded everyday with so much social information that our brains need shortcuts. Over time we are exposed to data that are consistent with our stereotypes and data that contradict them. We are simply more likely to notice and remember those things that confirm our expectations. Our trust in the accuracy of our own perception and memory then leads us to conclude that we have encountered far more confirmations and far fewer refutations than is actually true. This strengthens the perceived correlation and the relevant stereotype and makes us even more likely to notice future confirming examples.

A third factor that contributes to illusory correlations is the **availability heuristic**. This heuristic reflects our tendency to base our decisions and beliefs on images that most readily come to mind. It is easier for most of us to think of examples of dishonest politicians than honest ones. The reason of course is that stories of dishonesty in politics are widely and repeatedly publicized. The same process causes many people to believe that airplane travel is far more dangerous than is actually the case. Reports of plane crashes are heavily reported and therefore easily accessible in our memories. Images of safe plane trips are far less vivid and therefore have less of an effect on our beliefs. Similarly, honest or selfless acts by politicians seldom make headlines. What's more, we often hear about politicians' dishonesty but we seldom hear about a neighbor who cheats on his taxes. Again we end up misperceiving associations between events that we observe. Just as we exaggerate the link between airplane travel and danger, we exaggerate the link between politics and dishonesty.

Finally, illusory correlations are maintained by **self-fulfilling prophecies**. When we hold a stereotype, we are usually unaware that our beliefs actually affect our own behaviors and that our behavior sometimes makes it difficult or impossible for us to refute a stereotype. For example, imagine holding a

Although more bicycle riders have died in recent years than air travelers, the availability heuristic causes us to exaggerate the link between airplane travel and danger. *(Bureau of Transportation Statistics)*

stereotype that people who drive sports cars are inconsiderate drivers. When you see a sports car in your rearview mirror, you expect that the driver will drive aggressively and follow too closely. If the driver of the sports car does this, your stereotype is confirmed and strengthened. If not, you may unconsciously lift your foot from the gas pedal just enough to slow down slightly so that the driver behind you closes in. Although your own behavior played a role in what occurs next (i.e., the driver behind you closes in), you are not aware of this and your stereotype is confirmed. Research suggests that we do in fact tend to act preemptively when prompted by our own stereotypes. If we expect that members of some specific group tend to be hostile, our behavior when interacting with members of that group will likely send nonverbal signals that we are intimidated or uncomfortable. These signals may then affect the behavior of others without any awareness on our part.

PREJUDICE AND DISCRIMINATION

Although stereotypes are rooted in normal cognitive processes, they do not exist in a vacuum. Our beliefs and thoughts about members of various groups

If you believe that people who drive sports cars are inconsiderate drivers, you might act on that stereotype when you encounter a sports car on the road. *(Wikipedia)*

Stereotype Threat

Stereotypes can affect the behavior of those who are targets of generalized beliefs. Claude Steele identified a phenomenon he called stereotype threat which occurs because people are aware of stereotypes about their own groups. Examples concerning academic performance are particularly striking. Steele and his colleagues found that when black college students thought they were taking a test that measured intellectual ability, their scores were lower than when the same test was presented as something other than an ability test. Another study showed that simply asking black students to report their race was sufficient to lower their test performance.

Similar findings have emerged with respect to gender stereotypes. Researchers Kelly Danaher and Christian Crandall studied data from the Advanced Placement Calculus exam that high school students take to earn college credit. They estimated that simply requiring students to report their gender after completing the exam rather than at the start of the exam would increase the number of women receiving college credit in calculus by 4,700 each year.

Steele noted that even very subtle reminders of a stereotype about one's group can cause immediate anxiety, distracting attention from the task at hand. In the long term, stereotype threat can cause members of stereotyped groups to disengage from academic activities, further hindering performance.

are inextricably linked with our emotions and behaviors toward those groups. **Prejudice** refers to primarily negative emotions that we feel toward different groups. **Discrimination** occurs when we treat people differently based on their membership in those groups. Whereas stereotyping involves placing people into categories, prejudice and discrimination emerge when we begin to care one way or another about those categories. All of these processes can occur rather quickly. We form mental categories quite easily, and once we have done this, it takes little time for us to begin valuing (or denigrating) some categories more than others.

Once groups have been identified and stereotypes have been created, competition between groups often breeds prejudice and becomes a trigger for conflict. In a classic study of intergroup conflict, a famous social psychologist named Muzafer Sherif and his colleagues studied a group of boys who came together at a summer camp held in Robbers Cave State Park in Oklahoma. None of the boys knew each other prior to the study, nor did they know that they were participating in an experiment. Having first received permission from the boys' parents and prior to the boys' arrival at the camp, Sherif assigned the boys to two different groups. Neither of the groups was aware that the other group existed until a week after arriving at camp. During that first week, each group engaged in typical summer camp activities such as camping and hiking.

After each group had established its own identity, the groups were made aware of each other's existence and were placed in competition on a variety of activities during which they could earn points by defeating the other group. Very quickly, extreme animosity developed between the groups and the repercussions were startling. The hostility became so severe that the boys even ransacked each others' living quarters. Sherif and his colleagues tried a number of strategies to eliminate the intergroup conflict, including eliminating competition, but their efforts failed until they assigned projects whose successful completion would require cooperation between the groups. Instituting such **superordinate goals** was the only approach that reduced the animosity between the groups, and it was remarkably effective.

Conflict such as that observed in the Robbers Cave study is common when groups are in competition—or even if they just believe they are in competition—for resources that are in limited supply. In the case of the boys at the summer camp, the competition was real and the groups were competing for rewards that were in limited supply. The same often occurs in real life when we perceive that a gain in resources enjoyed by a group other than our own constitutes a loss for our own group. As an example, consider the negative view that some people hold concerning affirmative action policies that encourage the hiring of members of underrepresented groups. Some perceive such policies as unfair because the number of available jobs is limited, so policies favoring one group promote a sense of competition and potential hostility. In some cases, the perception that progress for one group represents a loss to another group, becomes a sense of absolute deprivation, particularly among those who are personally affected. In other cases, people experience a sense of relative deprivation. That is, they see members of another group apparently gaining ground and as a consequence they feel threatened. Even if they do not experience any personal difficulties or deprivation, the sense that their group as a whole is losing ground can promote hostility toward the other group.

Much research on prejudice has involved the use of minimal groups—groups created by researchers based on some minor and arbitrary characteristic. Such research has consistently illustrated how easy it is to create artificial groups that quickly inspire and motivate prejudice and discrimination that is all too real. In one famous illustration of this phenomenon, Jane Elliott, an elementary school teacher in Iowa in the 1960s, developed a class exercise for her third grade students. One morning she told her third grade class that the students with blue eyes were superior to the students with brown eyes. The blue-eyed students then enjoyed special privileges for the day, such as extended recess and extra food during lunch; the brown-eyed students were belittled. Surprisingly quickly, the blue-eyed students adopted their roles as superior class members and began mistreating brown-eyed students—even those who had been their friends prior to the exercise. Jane Elliott took careful steps to reverse the process by giving the brown-eyed students a chance at superiority as well. This exercise raised a great deal of controversy but illustrated how readily people come to identify with an ingroup and how quickly they can begin to disparage outgroup members, even when the characteristic distinguishing the groups is as trivial and arbitrary as eye color.

Subsequent researchers more formally employed what came to be known as the **minimal group paradigm**. Just as Jane Elliott used the arbitrary characteristic of eye color, researchers used a variety of trivial differences to create group identities. This research shows that people can very easily be made to perceive others as either ingroup or outgroup members and that once such a distinction is made, people tend to greatly exaggerate the differences between the groups and allocate more resources to members of their ingroup. One study even showed that activating a specific group identity is unnecessary in that even brief exposure to words such as "we" or "us" can bias people toward ingroup favoritism.

Such prejudice and discrimination occur between individuals and small groups but they also occur on a broad scale and sometimes are even formalized in the structure of various organizations. Historically in the United States, policies prevented women and ethnic minorities from entering many occupations and even from voting. Even today, some fraternities, sororities, and other social organizations prohibit people of some religious and ethnic groups from becoming members. Discrimination is also an everyday event that can occur on a much more subtle level. Teachers sometimes unintentionally treat students

Blood Sugar and Prejudice?

In a very interesting recent study, researchers observed that stereotyping and prejudice can be affected by one's immediate blood sugar level. Matthew Gaillot and his colleagues noted that suppression of prejudice requires self-control, and self-control processes cause the body to consume glucose. Half of the participants in this study drank lemonade sweetened with sugar, which increased their blood glucose levels; the other half drank lemonade with artificial sweetener. The participants then viewed a photograph of an adult male whom they believed to be a homosexual and wrote a brief essay about a typical day in the person's life. Compared with those who consumed artificial sweetener, people who had consumed sugar wrote essays containing fewer stereotypes about homosexuals. In addition, after consuming sugar, even those participants who were already highly prejudiced were less likely to make derogatory statements about homosexuals.

differently based on their gender or ethnicity, and employers sometimes hesitate to hire older people even when their age would not limit their ability to perform the necessary tasks. The list of examples is endless. In the next section, we will briefly examine two specific and familiar types of prejudice and discrimination.

SEXISM AND RACISM

As noted in the introduction to this chapter, it is difficult to think separately about the concepts of stereotyping, prejudice, and discrimination. These three phenomena often go hand in hand as the mental categorization that character- izes stereotyping easily leads to different feelings toward different groups and eventually to differential treatment of members of those groups. Two of the most common and important examples of this pattern are racism and sexism. In each case the distinctions between social categories can quickly lead to members of some groups being valued more than others and treated accordingly.

Sexism

Sexism refers to biased emotions and treatment based on people's gender, but this bias begins with gender stereotyping. If you are old enough to be reading this book it is likely that you are quite familiar with many stereotypes about men and women. Very early in life we become aware of our own biological sex and that of others, and we quickly become acquainted with the types of behaviors that society expects from people of each sex. For example, women are often expected to be nurturing and supportive, whereas men are expected to be strong and independent. Most of us also learn through the consequences of own behavior and by observing others' behavior that there can be unpleasant social penalties for violating societal gender roles. Like many stereotypes, beliefs about gender are often rooted in men's and women's traditional roles in society. Throughout our lives we observe people in all kinds of roles, and we come to expect that certain types of people belong in certain roles. Often we assume that people gravitate toward particular roles based on personal preference and that stereotypes reflect these preferences. We may fail to recognize that long term social structure and related stereotypes may tend to assign people to various roles based on their gender. That is, the stereotypes reflect social structure as much as any innate gender differences, and people choose roles accordingly.

As is often the case with stereotyping, our expectations for people based on their biological sex can lead to self-fulfilling prophecies. New parents respond differently to their babies depending on whether those babies are boys or girls. Parents of newborn boys tend to perceive their babies as bigger and stron- ger, whereas parents of girls tend to perceive their babies as smaller and more delicate—even when there are no actual differences in weight or other relevant physical characteristics. These differential perceptions based on sex lead to differential treatment as the children develop. Over time, the degree to which differences between boys and girls arise from natural tendencies or from subtle encouragement from adults becomes less clear.

Once we have acquired expectations for what is appropriate for members of each sex, these expectations play a powerful role in how we view others' behavior as well as our own. An interesting point about gender stereotypes is that unlike most stereotypes that are generalized beliefs about what members of a group are like, gender stereotypes also provide a guide for what men and women are supposed to be. Consequently we often feel that we must conform to stereotypical gender roles, and we fear repercussions if our behavior diverges too greatly from what others expect. Whether it is a second-grade boy being ridiculed by his peers for behaving in a stereotypically feminine way or a woman business executive derided for expressing authority and power, the consequences of failing to conform to gender stereotypes can be quite punitive.

Racism

Racism also refers to biased emotions and behavior, but here the prejudice and discrimination are based on racial differences often associated with skin color and other physical attributes. The United States has a long history of racial prejudice and discrimination, beginning with decades of slave importation early in the nation's history. The century that followed the elimination of institutionalized slavery at the conclusion of the Civil War was characterized by widespread and blatant discrimination against African Americans. The civil rights movement that began in the 1960s triggered a gradual reduction in public acceptance of racism, and expressions of racial prejudice that had previously been a rather typical part of everyday life became abhorrent to more and more people. Contemporary surveys about racial attitudes suggest that levels of racial prejudice and support for discrimination have declined greatly over the past several decades. But has racial bias really declined?

When people use the term racism in everyday life they often mean blatant, old-fashioned expressions of bias. When we think of racist acts, what likely comes to mind are images of white people shouting racial epithets at black people. Of course, racism has never been limited to verbal insults, but such public expressions used to be far more common than they are today. Although some might conclude that racial prejudice is largely a thing of the past, research suggests that racism has simply become more subtle.

Several theories propose that although public expressions of racism have become increasingly unacceptable, prejudice and negative emotions remain. In other words, legal and social prohibitions have reduced the prevalence of racist behavior, but internal negative emotions toward certain groups change more slowly. As time goes on and racism becomes less and less acceptable, people become more motivated to see themselves—and for others to see them—as unprejudiced. The clash between real negative emotions and prohibitions against expressing those emotions results in subtle expressions of bias. For example, rather than seeing blacks as unworthy of social and economic advancement, a person with subtle prejudice might feel that blacks are progressing too quickly and without enough effort of their own. The subtle racist would deny possessing racist attitudes, but expresses persistent negative emotions in ways that can be justified with non-prejudiced explanations.

What this means is that the shift toward public condemnation of overt racism has led many people to suppress or deny their negative emotions. Researchers interested in examining racial prejudice thus face the particularly difficult task of measuring something that is not directly observable and that most people are highly motivated to hide. In recent years, researchers have begun to use strategies to measure implicit prejudicial attitudes. Our implicit attitudes are those that are not directly obvious to others and are often hidden even from our own awareness. We may have little conscious prejudice against members of a particular group, but our minds may still harbor mental associations between that group and various negative characteristics. In contrast to explicit surveys that simply ask people to report their conscious attitudes, implicit attitude tests assess less obvious attitudes by using computers to measure how quickly people respond to positive and negative words after seeing a member of a target group. For example, a person taking such a test might see a photograph of an African American displayed on the computer screen. The computer then measures whether the person subsequently responds more quickly to positive or negative words. All this happens very quickly with the intention of revealing hidden mental associations rather than conscious attitudes. A growing body of research shows that people's implicit attitudes often diverge from the explicit attitudes they report on surveys.

Racism certainly continues to play a role in national discourse, and social psychologists continue to pursue greater understanding of its roots and consequences. Legal and social changes over several decades have served to reduce public expressions of racial prejudice, and there has been a clear shift toward public abhorrence of overt racism. The degree to which these changes reflect dramatic reductions in actual prejudice or merely suppression of overt racism is an issue of ongoing debate. Like most questions about human behavior, the answer most likely lies somewhere in the middle—overt racism has declined over time but prejudice between racial groups is far from a thing of the past.

REDUCING PREJUDICE AND DISCRIMINATION

Most social psychologists (and many other people) agree that prejudice and discrimination are social problems that should be overcome. Therefore researchers have sought not only to understand the causes and consequences of prejudice but have also explored ways to curtail it. In the 1950s, Gordon Allport proposed that prejudice and discrimination between groups would decline if people came into contact with members of other social groups under productive circumstances. He proposed that intergroup contact by itself would not be sufficient to reduce prejudice; to be effective, the contact would need to meet several criteria. First, the groups would need to have equal status. If one group had authority over the other, prejudice might actually increase. Second, the contact should include tasks that require the groups to cooperate in order to achieve success. Recall from the Robbers Cave study described earlier in this chapter that the researchers had little success mitigating the animosity between the two groups of boys until they introduced superordinate goals that could not be reached unless the groups worked together toward the shared objective. To reduce prejudice, it is also important that members of the two groups have individual interactions with one another and that contact between the groups is supported and promoted by some authority so it becomes perceived as normal.

As you might suspect, creating opportunities for intergroup contact that meet all of Allport's proposed criteria can be exceptionally difficult. Outside of research laboratories, it is seldom possible to exercise so much control over people's environments. However, this approach to reducing prejudice and discrimination has informed a variety of strategies, including something referred to as the jigsaw classroom. The **jigsaw classroom** is a strategy used primarily with school children and involves cooperative learning and superordinate goals. The method gets its name from comparisons with a jigsaw puzzle where each individual piece is part of a bigger picture. In the jigsaw classroom, each student must learn a portion of the material and then teach that material to the other students. Each student's success is therefore dependent on the help of other students, but each student also plays a role in the success of others. Research has shown that this strategy can be effective for reducing prejudice and also for improving relationships and increasing self-esteem.

SUMMARY

In this chapter we have learned that the way we think about people is ultimately linked with the way we feel about and treat those people. We have learned that stereotypical beliefs start out as mental categorizations that lead us to perceive some people as ingroup members and others as part of our outgroup. Once this occurs, ordinary human cognitive biases serve to solidify our beliefs about different groups. We may then come to value some groups more than others, which in turn causes us to treat them differently. Often we are not even aware that our beliefs and expectations affect both our own behavior and that of others. Efforts to reduce prejudice between groups have been most successful when they have required members of different groups to work together toward a common goal. Great progress has been made toward understanding and reducing prejudice, but great hurdles remain.

Further Reading

Allport, Gordon W. *The Nature of Prejudice*. Oxford, England: Addison-Wesley, 1954.

Nelson, Todd D. (Ed). *Handbook of Prejudice, Stereotyping, and Discrimination*. New York: Psychology Press, 2009.

Stangor, Charles (Ed.) *Stereotypes and Prejudice: Essential Readings. Key Readings in Social Psychology*. New York: Psychology Press, 2000.

CHAPTER 5

RELATIONSHIPS

Relationships are almost as vital to human beings as water and food. They fuel our happiness and allow us to tolerate and even to flourish in the face of daily stresses and adversity. In contrast, a lack of relationships in one's life can be devastating. Chronic loneliness in adults has been linked to depression, anxiety, heart problems, and substance abuse. As painful as loneliness is for adults, it can be even more harmful for infants and children. In fact, babies deprived of human contact and interaction may experience problems with physical and emotional development—even if their sustenance needs are adequately satisfied. In some cases, babies even die as a result of such deprivation.

The importance of relationships often becomes most clear when social connections are absent. One vivid illustration of how harmful being isolated from other human beings can be occurs when prison inmates are placed in solitary confinement. When in solitary, prisoners spend days, weeks, or even years without any social contact, often suffering intense psychological consequences such as depression, psychosis, or even suicidal thoughts. These effects make solitary confinement one of the worst punishments a person can face.

Dennis Charney, a psychiatrist who has studied human resilience, found it particularly enlightening to interview Vietnam War veterans who were held for years in solitary confinement as prisoners of war. He wondered why some men survived the experience without lasting mental health problems while others suffered severe psychological impairment. One major factor in maintaining psychological health was having contact with other POWs. Some POWs he

Some POWs studied by psychiatrist Dennis Charney were so motivated to connect with others that despite being kept in isolated concrete cells, they found a way to communicate with each other by tapping on the walls. *(Shutterstock)*

studied were so motivated to connect with others that despite being kept in isolated concrete cells, they found a way to communicate with each other by tapping on the walls. Using an intricate tap code to spell out words and sentences, these men shared their lives with one another. They were able to express mutual caring, learn from each other, and overcome feelings of loneliness. This unusual form of communication and the relationships it facilitated were critical in allowing the prisoners not only to survive, but also to grow during their incarcerations.

Fortunately most of us will never have to endure the horror of solitary confinement, but the relationship development process is familiar to us all. In this chapter we will look at how psychologists define relationships, consider how people come together and stay together, and examine the concepts of love and sexuality.

RELATIONSHIP DEVELOPMENT

Psychologists define relationships in much the same way as anyone else—a **relationship** is simply a social connection between two or more people. The definition may seem elementary, but the nature and course of relationships can be quite complex. Consider the many types of relationships that are possible and what sparks those relationships. How is your relationship with your best friend different from your relationship with someone you only see in class? Why are some relationships closer than others? Why do some relationships last a lifetime while others fade? What brings two people together in the first place? These questions are challenging, but they are exactly the types of questions that social psychologists seek to answer. In this section, we will explore some of the factors that influence relationship development.

Proximity

The first ingredient in the formation of any relationship is proximity or physical closeness to another person. Before any other factors come into play, relationship development requires initial contact between people. Proximity is so fundamental that we often are not even aware of its importance. Think again about your best friend. How did you meet? Perhaps your friend was in your homeroom, attended the same camp, or had the locker next to yours at school. For whatever reason, you were probably in the same place at the same time.

In a now famous study, Leon Festinger and his colleagues examined the impact of proximity on relationships by examining friendships between people living in the same apartment building. It turned out that where a person lived in the building mattered. Close neighbors were most likely to develop friendships whereas people living on different floors were least likely to be friends. However, living close to someone was not the only important factor. Interestingly, people who lived near common areas such as the staircase and mailboxes were more likely to have friends from other parts of the building. Their popularity makes sense when you consider how many people would pass by their apartments every day. By virtue of their location in the building, they crossed paths with more people than most and therefore had the

Before any other factors come into play, relationship development requires initial contact between people. *(Mathias Klang. Wikipedia)*

opportunity to develop relationships with people who did not necessarily live right next door.

Mere Exposure/Familiarity

Proximity is the first critical factor in relationship development, but physical closeness certainly does not guarantee that a relationship will form. It is very likely that you have met many people with whom you did not become friends. Moreover, you may not have developed much of a relationship with your best friend on your first encounter. More likely, your relationship probably evolved over the course of many encounters. Because we tend to like things that are familiar, repeated contact with someone increases the likelihood that a relationship will form. This phenomenon is called the **mere-exposure effect**, an effect that is quite easily observed in everyday life. Have you ever gone to a restaurant, looked at the whole menu and then ordered the same thing you always order? Maybe you have chosen one class over another solely because you were familiar with the teacher. Perhaps you can think of a song that you like. It could well be that you did not particularly care for this song the first time you heard it, but grew to like it after hearing it a number of times. Hundreds of studies have shown that when people are repeatedly exposed to a stimulus they will generally rate that stimulus more positively than an unfamiliar one.

Researchers Richard Moreland and Scott Beach illustrated the exposure effect in a very interesting study. They arranged for several different women to sit in on a large lecture course. To the actual students in the class, the visiting women appeared to be students as well. They sat quietly, took notes, and did not interact with anyone, so any impressions that the other students had about these women would be based on nothing more than their mere presence. The only real difference between the women was that they attended different numbers of class sessions. At the end of the term, the researchers asked students to look at pictures of the women and rate them on different characteristics such as attractiveness and intelligence. They found that the more classes a woman attended, the more positively the other students rated her. In other words, even without saying a word, the women the students saw more often were rated more positively. Now think back to the proximity study conducted by Leon Festinger. It is likely that mere exposure also contributed to the development of friendships in the apartment building that was the site of the study. Neighbors tend to see each other repeatedly, and we tend to feel more positively about familiar people.

Reciprocity

By now you are probably thinking more deeply about the initial elements of relationship development. Proximity and familiarity are both significant, but forming a good relationship requires something more, and one essential ingredient

Proximity and Familiarity in the Age of Technology

The Internet has made it necessary for social psychologists to rethink the role of proximity and familiarity in relationship development. Not so long ago, people could establish relationships only with people that they met in person or spoke with on the telephone. Now, because of the Internet, it is possible and even easy to contact people from all over the world and to develop relationships without ever meeting someone face to face. People meet on social networking sites, in chat rooms, and through online gaming. People can also become more familiar with one another through the frequency of their Internet contacts. By just "friending" people on Facebook, you can be privy to their deepest thoughts (or their most random and pointless thoughts). Once you meet someone online, you can "chat" with and thereby become more familiar with that person. Theoretically, relationships can form and deepen in this way in much the same way as they would in "real life." The roles of proximity and familiarity still hold, but the contacts are virtual rather than physical.

is affinity, which boils down to liking someone. If, for instance, you repeatedly meet a person whom you find to be quite rude, you will probably dislike that person even more over time. Therefore, developing a friendship or other close relationship depends on liking someone. And because we tend to like people who like us, another very simple part of liking someone is knowing that the person likes you. We tend to like others who like us. Knowing that someone feels positively about us can be quite rewarding and, the positive feelings we experience become associated with that person. Furthermore, it is human nature to want to give something back when we receive something. When someone gives you a birthday card, for example, you would probably feel bad if you did not reciprocate. The same tendency toward reciprocation occurs when you realize that someone else likes you. On some level, people often feel compelled to like those who like them.

As you read this, however, you might be wondering how this "I like you if you like me" pattern applies to the age old dating strategy of "playing hard-to-get?" The assumption underlying this strategy is that in order to attract someone you should pretend that the person is no more special to you than anyone else. Appearing too eager supposedly will turn the other person off, so the opposite tactic of playing hard-to-get is supposed to pique the other person's interest. But just as we like those who like us, we dislike those who dislike us. Therefore playing hard-to-get would probably do more harm than good because it sends a message of disinterest and may also convey dislike.

Research in social psychology has illustrated that playing hard-to-get may be effective but only under certain conditions. Paul Eastwick and his colleagues examined attraction in a speed-dating context. The researchers studied more than 150 participants who each had 4-minute "dates" with several people. After these brief encounters, the participants rated their dates. The researchers found that "unselective romantic desire" was a turn-off for the participants. That is, people were not attracted to others who seemed attracted to everyone. It is obvious from this result that playing easy-to-get was not an effective strategy. So does this mean you should play hard-to-get? The best answer here is "sort of." What these and other researchers have found is that the most effective strategy is being selectively hard-to-get. In other words, people are attracted to others who like them but are hard for others to get. We like to feel special and when we do, we tend to reciprocate in kind.

Reciprocity is not only a part of what draws people together, it is also an integral part of strengthening long-term relationships. Think again about your relationship with your best friend. You and your friends probably know more about each other than other people know. How did you learn so much about one another? The probable explanation is that you and your friend began by talking about mundane things, like the weather or a book you had both read. When you realized that you were comfortable talking with each other about less personal topics, one of you probably disclosed something a little more intimate. The other then probably reciprocated with some personal information, and so on. It is in this way that we progress from having acquaintances to having meaningful friendships.

Similarity

Think about the things you talk about when you meet a new person at a party. Do you talk about all the ways in which you are different from that other person? Probably not. You are most likely trying to find what makes the two of you similar. You might talk about a teacher you both had, a movie you have both seen, or a sport you both love. Chances are that the more you find in common, the longer your conversation lasts; the longer your conversation lasts, the more likely it is that you will talk again or even plan to do something together. When you spend time with someone who is similar to you, you are more likely to do things that you both enjoy, and you are also more likely to feel that the other person understands and respects you. Similarity, and the behavior that evolves from it, can deepen your relationship with that person.

Just as reciprocity plays a role both in the formation and strengthening of relationships, similarity between people influences relationships in the short and long term. Think about the divisions that arise between people when politics and religion become topics of conversation. We can often tolerate and even appreciate what makes someone different from us if we do not see those differences as being very important. But when others have different core values from us or are different in ways that we think are very important, it becomes much harder to form and maintain close relationships with them. Thus, the old adage "birds of a feather flock together" represents how relationships generally work.

If you have heard the saying "opposites attract," you may be feeling a little confused at this point. That cliché suggests that we like people who are different from us. But while it is true that spending time with someone who is very different from you can be interesting and exciting, imagine how hard it might be to develop and then maintain a close relationship with someone whose values or interests are very different from your own.

Aside from the comfort and familiarity that come with being around people who are like us, we also tend to make positive assumptions about people who are similar to us. If you consider yourself to be a smart and interesting person, it would make sense for you to assume that someone who is similar to you is also smart and interesting. Research has revealed just such a pattern. In a classic study on attraction and similarity, Donn Byrne had participants review an attitude survey that was supposedly completed by an anonymous student. The more closely the attitudes of the anonymous student aligned with those of the participant, the more likely it was for the participant to report liking

Some say that opposites attract, but the old adage "birds of a feather flock together" more closely represents how relationships work. *(Wikipedia. Courtesy of Gideon)*

the anonymous student. Additionally, participants rated those with similar attitudes to themselves as more intelligent, more informed about current events, more moral, and better adjusted overall.

Similarity attracts us to others for several reasons. It is easier to spend time with someone who shares our common interests and values, and doing so is enjoyable and makes us feel respected and valued. Furthermore, since we tend to make positive assumptions about people who are similar to us, we will probably like them not only for who they are, but also for who we assume them to be. If you have ever tried to "fit in" with other people or succumbed to "peer pressure," then you know how important similarities in relationships can be. Someone different doesn't easily fit in; the same goes for someone who does not give in to peer pressure exerted by most or all other members in a group he or she belongs to or would like to belong to.

Physical Attractiveness

In an ideal world, a person's appearance would not affect how others feel about that person. But as much as we profess that we should "never judge a book by

A single positive trait can inspire a "halo effect" that makes us assume the person has many other positive traits. The people looking at the attractive woman in the foreground of this photo are likely to assume she may be interesting, well educated, have a good sense of humor, or other positive characteristics. *(Wikipedia)*

its cover," most of us do. In other words, looks matter. Just as we tend to make favorable assumptions about people who are similar to us, we tend to make all kinds of positive assumptions about people who are physically attractive. This tendency to identify one positive trait in a person and then assume the person has many other positive traits is known as the **halo effect**. Interestingly, the halo effect can also work in the opposite direction—observing one negative trait can prompt us to make a number of negative assumptions about someone.

The halo effect can often be observed in political contests. In a study of Canadian elections, researchers found that physically attractive candidates received nearly three times more votes than unattractive candidates. But this phenomenon is clearly not limited to Canada. Many historians believe that appearance played an enormous part in John F. Kennedy's election to the presidency of the United States of America in 1960. A much less experienced candidate than his opponent Richard Nixon, Kennedy was not performing well in the polls until their first debate. Those who listened to the debate on the radio felt Nixon had won; those who watched the debate on television felt that Kennedy was the better candidate. Kennedy appeared healthier, more confident, and more attractive than Nixon, and this debate changed the course of the election. Physical attractiveness can also have an impact on other social interactions, such as hiring decisions, altruistic behavior, academic grading, and even court verdicts and prison sentences. Interestingly, most people are unaware of having this bias toward attractive people and are even less aware of how heavily they are influenced by appearance.

You have probably heard the expression "beauty is in the eye of the beholder." This phrase implies that there is no consensus about attractiveness, and like many clichés, it bears little resemblance to real life. Numerous studies have shown that there is indeed a consensus about what an attractive face looks like and have also shown that the consensus applies regardless of the sex, race, culture, or age of the rater or the person being rated. Some studies have shown that even newborn babies prefer to look at attractive faces over unattractive ones. Given the findings of attractiveness research, it stands to reason that physical attractiveness would also impact the formation of relationships. The previous examples (e.g., the Canadian election study) demonstrate how influential the attractiveness of those being judged can be on the judges. But what about the other side of the coin? What about the people doing the judging?

With regard to elections or contests or other similar interactions, the appearance of the "judges" (e.g., voters) is not measured and doesn't particularly matter. Relationships, on the other hand, are affected by the attractiveness of both people. The **matching hypothesis**, which has been supported by many studies, suggests that people tend to enter into relationships with people they feel are similar to them in degree of attractiveness. So why is it that most of us do not seek out relationships with people who are more attractive than we are?

The pressure to maintain and improve our appearance can lead to problematic behaviors, including eating disorders like bulimia, which is characterized by an excessive concern with weight. After eating, people suffering from bulimia will often induce vomiting to purge unwanted calories. *(Shutterstock)*

One answer may be fear of rejection. Rather than shoot for the stars and lose, we tend to pursue relationships with people who seem attainable.

Beauty definitely has a lot of benefits, but it can be a mixed blessing. Beautiful people are often unsure of whether the positive feedback they get from others is based on their abilities, other good qualities, or solely on appearance. They also tend to feel more pressure to maintain and improve their appearance. Such pressure can lead to problematic behaviors, including steroid use, excessive plastic surgery, and eating disorders. Despite all the advantages of beauty, it does not ensure happiness. In fact, happiness later in life seems to have little to do with one's appearance when young. The good news is that the more frequently we see someone, the more attractive that person appears to us. While there is certainly a continuum of physical attractiveness and being physically attractive can help one to make a good first impression, people all along the continuum can be attractive to others and may appear to become more attractive over time, at least to the people in their lives who matter most.

ROMANTIC RELATIONSHIPS
Gender Differences in Romantic Attraction
The factors already mentioned that influence interpersonal attraction apply to both men and women. Additionally, both men and women report valuing similar personality characteristics in their romantic partners, including a good sense of humor, kindness, dependability, and a pleasant disposition. However, as you might suspect, there are gender differences in romantic attraction as well. Heterosexual men and women do not always look for identical qualities in their mates. For instance, men tend to be attracted to younger, physically attractive, sexually inexperienced women; women tend to be drawn to older, ambitious, intelligent, and financially stable men. Men also tend to want to have more frequent sex with a variety of partners whereas women tend to be more discriminating in their partnering.

One controversial perspective regarding the different preferences of men and women is derived from the theory of evolution. According to the evolutionary perspective, people are biologically driven to procreate and to ensure the survival of their children. This drive pushes us toward mates who increase our chances of achieving this positive outcome. For men this means being most attracted to women who are likely to be highly fertile. Furthermore, because men do not have to invest much time or energy in reproduction, it is to their advantage to have sex with many women to increase the number of potential offspring. This theory may explain why men often seek to mate with young and attractive women. Youth and attractiveness are cues that a woman is healthy and fertile enough to become pregnant and carry a fetus to term.

The evolutionary perspective further predicts that women will be more discerning than men in their mate selection. Women are not biologically able to have as many children as men, so it is in their best interests to consider quality over quantity when seeking out mates. Therefore, women search for men who have the means or at least the potential to provide for them and their child(ren). Furthermore, because women invest nine months in a single pregnancy, having sex with many men does not contribute to the procreation goal.

Although evolutionary theory provides some explanation for mate preferences, many psychologists argue that there are simpler explanations for the mating habits of men and women. For instance, women may seek men with money if they do not have the same access to financial resources as men. In fact, in cultures where women have greater direct access to financial security, women

Attachment and Relationships

So far we have examined some general things that people look for in others when forming relationships. But, is everyone equally able to have close relationships? Are there personal characteristics that might influence our ability to have close positive relationships with others? According to developmental psychologists, there are differences even among infants in the types of attachment bonds they develop with parents or primary caregivers. Early attachment appears to be influenced both by an infant's inborn temperament and by the degree of safety and responsiveness provided by the primary caregivers. These early attachment styles seem to play a role in the children's romantic relationships later in life.

Studies suggest that there are three adult attachment styles that are closely related to infant attachment styles. The healthiest of these is the secure attachment style. People who have this style of attachment find it relatively easy to trust and become close to others, without being indiscriminately trusting. They are comfortable both with depending on others and having others depend on them, and they assume that others are basically good and trustworthy. Secure people tend to have happy, satisfying, and long-lasting relationships.

In contrast, people with avoidant or anxious attachment styles are more likely to have a hard time forming healthy and long-lasting relationships. People with an avoidant attachment style find it difficult to trust others and therefore keep their emotional distance. Despite a desire to be close, they find it very uncomfortable to allow anyone to know them very well. Unlike people with an avoidant style, those with an anxious attachment style deal with distrust by attempting to keep their relationship partners overly close. They tend to have dramatic relationships and find it difficult to believe that they are truly loved.

Attachment tendencies are rooted in early childhood development. They can have a significant impact on the quality of a person's relationships throughout life.

rate the physical attractiveness of a potential mate as more important than do women in cultures which deny them economic power. Psychologists also point out that the similarities between the sexes are far greater than the differences. Both men and women state that the personality features of their mates are more important to them than physical attractiveness and financial potential.

Sexual Orientation

In the previous section we discussed heterosexual mating preferences; however, heterosexuality is not the only **sexual orientation**. In fact, there are three widely recognized orientations. Heterosexual people are attracted to sexual partners of the opposite sex; homosexual or gay people are attracted to partners of the same sex; and bisexual people are attracted to people of both sexes. Despite these seemingly distinct categories, most psychologists conceptualize sexual orientation on a continuum ranging from homosexuality to heterosexuality with bisexuality in the middle. Some research has indicated that most people are actually somewhat bisexual in that they have some level of sexual attraction to both sexes.

For centuries people have debated the causes and meanings of sexual orientation. While many still feel that homosexuality is a choice and is changeable, the preponderance of research has suggested that sexuality has a strong genetic component and is therefore at least somewhat biologically determined. In fact, although fewer than 10 percent of the people in the general population identify as homosexual, among identical twins, if one twin is gay the likelihood that the other twin is also gay is around 50 percent.

Some people believe that same-sex attraction is a mental illness; others believe that it is just one of many individual differences, like hair color or blood type. Until 1973, the American Psychiatric Association included homosexuality as a mental disorder in its diagnostic manual. Although this is no longer the case, non-heterosexual people do have higher rates of other mental disorders such as depression. Researchers speculate that these disorders are not caused by non-heterosexual orientations per se, but instead result from the discrimination and rejection gay and bisexual people face in their families and in society. In many respects, the romantic relationships that gay or bisexual people form with others are similar to those that develop among heterosexual people.

Love

Think about the people you love. Do you experience the same type of love for all of them? You probably recognize the differences in how you feel about these individuals quite quickly, which easily leads you to recognize that love has many dimensions. Psychologists have in fact identified a number of different types of love.

Same-sex couple holds hands at a marriage march. *(Wikipedia. Courtesy of Bastique)*

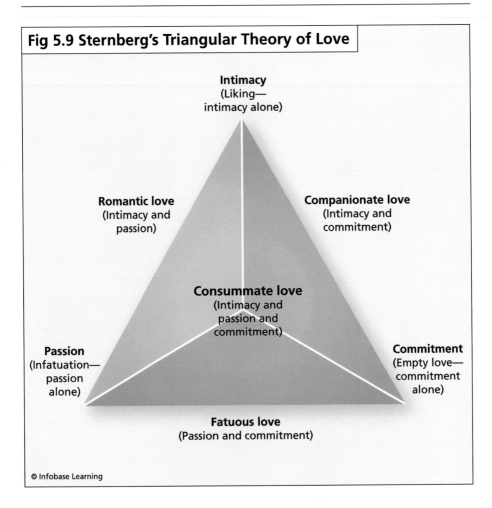

Fig 5.9 Sternberg's Triangular Theory of Love

Intimacy
(Liking—
intimacy alone)

Romantic love
(Intimacy and
passion)

Companionate love
(Intimacy and
commitment)

Consummate love
(Intimacy and
passion and
commitment)

Passion
(Infatuation—
passion
alone)

Commitment
(Empty love—
commitment
alone)

Fatuous love
(Passion and commitment)

© Infobase Learning

Robert Sternberg developed a **triangular theory of love** that includes three basic components of love: intimacy, passion, and commitment. Sternberg proposes that a person can experience each of these components in isolation or in some combination resulting in seven possible types of love. Infatuation, or passion-only love is probably better known as lust—an intense desire for another person that is based on physical attraction and sexual arousal. Passionate relationships may cause your heart to pound, your palms to sweat, and lead to the feeling of butterflies in your stomach. However, without other components of love, passionate relationships often fade over time. Many romantic relationships in Western society start out with only passion, incorporating intimacy and commitment as the relationship evolves.

Intimacy refers to emotional closeness and connectedness between two people. This type of closeness usually develops when two people share details of their lives and their innermost thoughts and feelings over time. Intimacy-only love is known as liking. Good friendships are an example because they usually involve a strong bond with another person, without sexual attraction and often with no long-term commitment. These relationships are characterized by mutual support and understanding. Friends may live in very different places and have very different lives but still keep in contact with one another and care deeply about each other.

Commitment is a conscious choice to be in a particular relationship for the long term. As is the case with passion and intimacy, you can have relationships that are based solely on commitment. In cultures where arranged marriages are the norm, people often initially enter a marriage with only a sense of commitment. The assumption in such cultures is that two people who are a good match for one another—an assumption generally determined by their parents based on variables like social class and religion—will develop intimacy and passion in their relationship over time. In Western society couples usually commit to one another only after they have a relationship that includes some level of intimacy

The End of a Relationship

We have discussed how relationships form and grow, but obviously many relationships end. For example, about 50 percent of marriages in the United States end in divorce. Some romantic relationships end because the priorities, interests, or values of the two partners shift and are no longer in close enough alignment. Others end because of what psychologist John Gottman refers to as the "four horsemen of the apocalypse," which are four negative behaviors that relationship partners may engage in that tend to lead to relationship demise. The first is criticism. Most people have complaints about their partners, but criticizing one's partner goes beyond complaining. Criticism entails attacking someone else's character rather than just asking that person to do something differently. The worst of the "horsemen," according to Gottman, is contempt which manifests itself through insults, name calling, eye rolling, mockery, and other psychologically abusive behaviors. When one partner has criticized and expressed contempt, the other partner usually becomes defensive. Defensiveness, the third "horseman," often involves defending oneself by reciprocating the criticism and contempt. The final "horseman" is stonewalling and involves the partners becoming emotionally distant as a means of avoiding conflict. The problem with this behavior is that although it helps to lower conflict, it also reduces the loving feelings in the relationship. Avoiding these toxic behaviors while maintaining and strengthening marital friendship is crucial for a happy union.

and passion. Such relationships, however, may deteriorate over time and lose their intimacy and passion. An example is marriages where the couple stays together "just for the children." The intimacy and passion fade, but the commitment remains. Similarly, adult siblings are often in commitment-only relationships with one another.

In addition to the single component types of love mentioned already, Sternberg identified varieties of love that reflect a blend of components. For instance, romantic love generally includes intimacy and passion without a long-term commitment whereas some marriages become companionate relationships that include intimacy and commitment but no passion. The ideal type of love between two romantic partners is known as consummate love and includes all three love components: intimacy, passion, and commitment. This is the type of love that most people strive for when looking for a life partner.

SUMMARY

This chapter examined people's fundamental need for relationships. Although some people might like to think that relationship development is a magical, even fated process, psychological research reveals that specific basic factors such as proximity, similarity, familiarity, and physical attractiveness have a powerful impact on the choices we make when establishing relationships with others and on whether those relationships thrive or wither. In addition to looking at these factors, this chapter has addressed the many possible types of love that can exist between people as well as the facts and myths regarding sexual orientation. Human relationships can be exceptionally complex, but psychological research has certainly given us a great deal of insight into that complexity.

Further Reading

Gottman, John M., and Nan Silver. *Why Marriages Succeed or Fail and How You Can Make Yours Last*. New York: Fireside Book, 1994.

Reis, Harry T., and Susan Sprecher. (Eds.) *Encyclopedia of Human Relationships* (Vols. 1–3). Thousand Oaks, Calif.: Sage Publications, 2009.

Sternberg, Robert J. "A Triangular Theory of Love." *Psychological Review* 93, no. 2 (1986): 119–135.

CHAPTER 6

PROSOCIAL AND ANTISOCIAL BEHAVIOR

INTRODUCTION

Social psychologists have long been interested in understanding human behavior at its best and worst. Prosocial behaviors are those intended to help other people, whereas antisocial behaviors are harmful to others. We often think of people as good or bad, and we tend to assume that people's tendencies to help or harm others are rooted in internal personality characteristics and general moral values. Although it is true that people differ in their moral values and some people help or harm more than others, research has demonstrated that prosocial and antisocial behaviors are highly influenced by the immediate context. In this chapter we'll look at some of the personal and situational factors that affect our tendencies toward altruism and aggression.

PROSOCIAL BEHAVIOR

At the time this book was being written, a horrific earthquake hit the poor island nation of Haiti in the Caribbean Sea. Much of the country's infrastructure was destroyed, and more than a quarter of a million people died. In the days, weeks, and months after the quake, countless people from all over the world worked in a variety of ways to help the people of Haiti survive and recover. Individuals donated money to provide food, shelter, and medical care to the victims of the quake. Many people organized drives to collect clothing and other necessities to send to people who had already been devastatingly poor before the quake and were now suffering even more. Thousands of people even went to Haiti to provide desperately needed services. When news of the Haitian earthquake spread across the world, people wanted to help—despite the fact that the victims were people they had never met and who would never be able to repay the favor.

Such altruistic behavior is certainly not limited to catastrophic events. Everyday, people help others in more typical and less public ways. A passenger on a bus or train gives up his or her seat to an elderly or disabled person. A family volunteers at a soup kitchen. A firefighter risks death to save someone he or she has never met. **Prosocial behaviors** are altruistic in nature, specifically because those engaging in prosocial behaviors help others rather than themselves. In essence, they involve unselfish acts intended to improve the lives or conditions of other people.

We often tend to focus on personal characteristics when we think about people who practice altruism and generosity. It seems relatively clear that some people are concerned about the well-being of others and therefore give of themselves to help people, whereas others are primarily preoccupied with their own self-interest. But like most generalizations about human behavior, this one is greatly oversimplified. Social psychologists have demonstrated that prosocial behaviors are affected by many factors. Most people engage in altruistic acts on some occasions and under some conditions and refrain from doing so at other times and under other conditions. Although the likelihood that a person will behave in a prosocial manner is certainly affected by personality, whether prosocial behavior occurs may also depend on who needs help, when, and why.

It is worth noting that a tendency to help others is not entirely restricted to humans. Altruistic behavior is also evident in other animals. For example, bees regularly sacrifice themselves for the good of the entire colony in a hive, and some birds issue warning calls to other members of their species when a predator is near—even though they jeopardize their own lives by doing so.

One aspect of prosocial behavior that intrigues evolutionary biologists and psychologists is that it appears, at least at first glance, to contradict the predictions of evolutionary theory. One of the core principles of evolutionary theory is that natural selection filters out the organisms that are least able to adapt to their environments. Conversely, characteristics that enhance the likelihood of an organism's survival and ability to produce offspring will be selected in a population over time. The key motivational prediction that follows is that an individual organism—human or otherwise—would not be expected to sacrifice its own resources or its own life to benefit others.

Despite the apparent contradiction, however, further examination reveals that altruistic behavior is in fact consistent with what evolutionary theory would predict. And this leads to a second interesting view of prosocial behavior—that the tendency to help others may be rooted in genetics. Richard Dawkins, a famous evolutionary biologist, speculated that the primary unit of evolution may not be the individual organism as we generally like to assume, but rather that organism's genes. This would mean that a member of a species could enhance the likelihood of his or her genes being passed to another generation by helping closely related members of that species to survive. This perspective leads to the prediction that people would be more likely to help close genetic relatives than more distantly related people. In fact, this appears to be the case. Researchers refer to this tendency as **kinship selection**, and in surveys people tend to report a greater willingness (particularly in life-or-death scenarios) to help close relatives such as siblings and parents than more distant relatives and friends. Even young children demonstrate this tendency. Of course this does not explain all instances of prosocial behavior, but it does help us to understand some of the conditions under which we are most likely to offer assistance.

Motives for Helping

We like to think of altruistic behavior (whether performed by others or by ourselves) as motivated by a selfless desire to help people. However this assumption may not always be accurate. In most cases when we help someone, we get some benefit from doing so. This fact has perpetuated a fascinating debate where some have questioned whether our motives to help others are ever truly selfless. The controversy concerning motives for prosocial behaviors is often referred to as the altruism-egoism debate. Those on the altruism side argue that humans often act simply for the betterment of others. Advocates of this position believe that it is possible for a person's behavior to be truly selfless. Opponents argue that seemingly altruistic behavior is often motivated not by selflessness but by some personal goal. Research has provided support for both perspectives.

One way we benefit from helping others is that doing so makes us feel good. And this "feel good" effect tends to promote subsequent altruistic behavior. Each time we behave prosocially and feel good about ourselves afterwards, the likelihood of helping again in the future increases. In behavioral psychology terms, helping is rewarded by a good feeling, something that then reinforces the behavior of helping. Research in this area also demonstrates that we are more likely to help when we are feeling bad about ourselves or our lives. Moreover, in such circumstances, prosocial actions can actually improve our mood. There is even evidence that helping others can make us feel better both mentally and physically. A group of researchers led by Jane Allyn Piliavin proposed that when we become aware of other people's suffering we experience an aversive state of arousal that we are motivated to eliminate. Helping those in need reduces our arousal and therefore improves our mood.

Helping others can be rewarding not only because it makes us feel good, but also because it makes us feel that we are behaving morally. After all, most of us learn early in life that we are supposed to help people when we can. Failing to help means abandoning this moral obligation and may cause us to experience guilt. It is also true, of course, that we are not always entirely honest (even with ourselves) about this motivation to help. Although we would like to believe that we are motivated by a desire to help others, there are times when we are actually more concerned that others see us as moral because most of us want others to think of us as good people. A body of fascinating research suggests that some pessimism about the inherent morality of prosocial behavior is warranted. The findings of this research suggest that people often adhere to moral standards promoting help for others only when they themselves will also benefit. Thus, people who can maintain an altruistic image without backing up this image

Narcissistic Altruism?

Although researchers have not been able to identify personality characteristics that consistently predict altruistic behavior, they have found that today's high school students volunteer more than students in the past did. In recent years, approximately three-quarters of high school seniors reported having volunteered in the previous year, compared with 64 percent in 1990. Surprisingly, today's adolescents are also more narcissistic on average than their 1990 counterparts. Research indicates that they tend to be more motivated by self-interest and less empathic than previous generations. Why would an increase in volunteerism among young people correspond with a rise in narcissism within the same population? Given that altruism is generally born from empathy, this association appears counterintuitive.

In their book *The Narcissism Epidemic: Living in the Age of Entitlement*, researchers Jean Twenge and W. Keith Campbell suggest that narcissism may lead to volunteerism because people find great egoistic value in making a difference in the world. That is, while the current generation of young people may still believe that it is important to help others, they are more motivated than their counterparts of past generations to put their stamp on the world. They may also be more prone to admit that their motivations are not purely selfless.

Twenge and Campbell also offer more pragmatic explanations for the increase in volunteerism among young people, specifically that many high schools have begun to require this. Such a requirement would naturally cause an uptick in community service. Additionally, some students volunteer in an effort to make themselves attractive candidates for admission to their preferred colleges. Paradoxically, self-interest promotes attending to the interests of others.

While it is likely that many of today's youth begin volunteering to benefit themselves, there is evidence that they may continue to volunteer even when some of those benefits are no longer relevant. In fact, it seems that the same narcissism that leads some people to help others may even be reduced by participation in required prosocial behavior.

with substance all too often fail to help because the appearance of helping has already been satisfied.

In contrast to these rather pessimistic perspectives on people's motives for helping others lies a more optimistic theory. Daniel Batson's empathy-altruism hypothesis proposes that people's empathy for others is the driving force behind much prosocial behavior. Empathy refers to our ability to see a situation from another person's perspective. When we feel empathy for someone, we are imagining what it would be like to be in that person's position and we therefore acquire a better understanding of what that person is experiencing. Batson in fact proposes that truly altruistic actions emerge from our empathy for others. When we see someone in need and allow ourselves to think about what it would be like and how it would feel to be in a similar state of need, we develop an altruistic desire to provide assistance. Our motivation is altruistic in the sense that it emerges from a desire to relieve someone else's discomfort rather than to make ourselves feel good. Batson thoroughly researched his proposal and found a great deal of support for the idea that people feeling empathy for someone in need are likely to help that person even when the costs of helping are relatively high. In contrast, people not experiencing empathy more often choose to leave a difficult situation rather than offering assistance.

When Is Help Likely?

In addition to the personal factors involved in prosocial behavior, there are also situational factors that affect the likelihood that helping will occur. In Chapter 1, you read about research conducted by Bibb Latane and John Darley on the bystander effect. This effect occurs when the responsibility to help someone is diffused among multiple people and when most of those people assume that someone else will help. The link with prosocial behavior is clear, and Latane and Darley extended their research to better understand the circumstances under which people are likely to help others in need. Within the context of this research, Latane and Darley identified a number of steps that progressively (and sequentially) lead to prosocial responses in any given situation.

The first step is recognition. If we don't notice that someone needs help, there is no chance that help will be forthcoming. This is not always as straightforward as it might seem. Often we fail to notice that a situation actually demands action on our part. Imagine, for example, that a man is lying unconscious on a sidewalk in your town. The first part of recognition means noticing that the unconscious man is there. As simple as this may sound, people are often so distracted by their own thoughts and other things going on around them that they fail to notice details in their environment. Once you notice the man on the sidewalk, you must also recognize that he needs assistance. This requires that you assess the situation and draw conclusions. Is the man intoxicated? Is he breathing? Is he bleeding? How you assess and interpret the man's condition affects your

If you see a man lying unconscious on a sidewalk, noticing that the man is there and that he requires assistance are prerequisites for providing help. *(Shutterstock)*

decision about whether to intervene or not. It is at this juncture that diffusion of responsibility often emerges and people begin to look to other people on the scene for cues about what if anything to do next. Unfortunately, everyone else is in a similar predicament and looking for the same cues, so uncertainty and inaction often prevail. These can also be contagious and are likely to affect new-comers to the scene as well.

But let's assume that you have cleared step one of this sequence and have recognized that this person lying in the street requires assistance. The second step is a shift to prosocial behavior—specifically a decision on your part that you are the person responsible for taking action. Now suppose that 50 other people on the scene have also reached this level. Here again, diffusion of responsibility can rear its head. Even when people are certain that someone needs help, they are less likely to offer assistance if other people are present. And the more people present, the less each of those people will feel individually responsible to help.

As you might expect, diffusion of responsibility generally occurs when we do not know the person in need of help or the other bystanders. If we know the victim, action is likely.

But let's return to our scenario of the unconscious (and anonymous) man lying on the sidewalk and the next step of Latane and Darley's progression. The final step in this sequence (like the first step) is twofold: deciding what to do and doing it. If you are like most people, you will choose an option that you can perform successfully. Prosocial behaviors in emergency situations can range from intense interventions such as administering CPR, to simply calling for police or an ambulance. But regardless of the specific action, it is likely to occur only after a step by step appraisal that can unfortunately be derailed at any of several points in the process.

One of these derailment factors is the degree to which we are under time constraints. John Darley and Daniel Batson conducted an intriguing study of the role of time pressure in prosocial behavior. The researchers asked seminary students to consider the story of the Good Samaritan, a Biblical parable that emphasizes the importance of helping people (even strangers) in need. The students were told to review the story in preparation for recording a brief talk on the subject. Students were then directed to another building where they would record their talks. Some of the students were told that they had ample time to get to the other building; others were told that they were running late. As they walked toward the other building, each participant passed a person slumped in a doorway with his eyes closed, and who only coughed and groaned. Among the students who were told they had ample time to get to the recording session in the other building, nearly two-thirds stopped to offer assistance. Among those who believed they were running late, only 10 percent stopped to help. The fact that the seminary students had just been reminded of the importance of helping others and were on their way to deliver a talk on that very subject had no effect on the likelihood that they would intervene—a very clear confirmation that time constraints can be very strong determinants of whether someone in need gets help.

Other factors also affect people's tendency to act prosocially. People in a small town are more likely to help others; people in a big city are less likely to do so. This is probably because big cities have more distractions that keep people from recognizing the needs of others; big cities also promote anonymity and diffusion of responsibility. Mood can also play a role. A variety of research suggests that sunshine, pleasant smells, imagining oneself on a tropical vacation, and many other mood-enhancing experiences tend to increase prosocial behavior. Interestingly, as noted earlier in this chapter, bad moods might sometimes promote prosocial behavior because people tend to learn that helping makes them feel good.

Who Helps and Who Gets Help?

The vast majority of research on prosocial behavior suggests that situational constraints play a much greater role than individual characteristics. There is little evidence of a single personality trait (or set of traits) that is consistent with prosocial behavior, regardless of the specific situation. Some people clearly choose to help far more frequently than others, but it is unclear what individual traits make frequent helpers different from those who help less often. Personality differences are less than noteworthy, but some research suggests that an interaction effect occurs where people with certain traits are more likely to help in certain situations. Nonetheless, it is not yet possible to draw firm conclusions about such interactions. Broadly speaking, the two personal characteristics that best predict prosocial behavior are the capacity to feel empathy and a well-developed capacity for moral reasoning. Consistent with the empathy-altruism hypothesis discussed earlier, people with a greater tendency to experience feelings of empathy when someone else is in need are more likely to help. Moral reasoning plays a similar role in that it tends to emphasize attention to others' needs rather than one's own. But as the study with the seminary students showed, this is not always the case.

Individual characteristics also increase the likelihood that a person will be the recipient of prosocial behavior. For example, unfair as it may seem, people who are physically attractive are more likely to be helped. Some fascinating studies show that even when other factors are held constant, good-looking people elicit more prosocial behavior than people who are less attractive. Another important characteristic is perceived responsibility for one's state of need. People are more likely to get help when they are not seen as responsible for their own predicaments. This is readily apparent when the person in need of assistance has a physical illness. For example, patients diagnosed with HIV are more likely to receive help from others if the disease was contracted through a blood transfusion than if it was contracted through sexual activity. The finding that people tend to help those who are not responsible for their problems is consistent with what is known as the just-world hypothesis. People are generally motivated to believe that the world is a just and fair place where people get what they deserve. When people suffer through no fault of their own, others feel a sense of injustice and are motivated to restore fairness by offering assistance.

So far in this chapter we have explored some of the factors that influence prosocial behavior. Research in this area is quite extensive, and the brief outline this chapter permits is simply an overview. As with any human behavior, it is often difficult or impossible to know how personal and environmental factors came together to determine a person's response to a particular situation. Human behavior is simply too complex for such analysis, so we must think in terms of broad human tendencies and consider what makes people generally more or less likely to engage in prosocial behavior. The same applies to antisocial behavior, which is discussed below.

ANTISOCIAL BEHAVIOR

Antisocial behaviors are those that are intended to harm other people. This is different from popular language usage in which people use the term *antisocial* to refer to individuals who keep to themselves and engage only reluctantly in social interaction. Such behavior might be more accurately described as asocial rather than antisocial. When social psychologists refer to antisocial acts, they are generally referring to behaviors involving various levels of aggression or even violence.

There is little question that among developed nations, the United States has one of the highest rates of violent crime. In 2008, the most recent year for which complete data are available, nearly 1.4 million violent crimes were reported in the United States. These included more than 14,000 murders and approximately 800,000 aggravated assaults. High-profile crimes such as the murderous rampages committed by students at Columbine High School in Littleton, Colorado,

School Shootings

High profile school shootings have drawn attention to the problem of aggression and violence among young people. On April 20, 1999, two students at Columbine High School in Colorado murdered twelve other students and a teacher at their school before committing suicide. On April 16, 2007, a student at Virginia Tech University murdered 32 people on campus before he too committed suicide. As horrific as these events are in and of themselves, they seem all the more tragic because the perpetrators and many of their victims were young people. Following such events, questions concerning what could have prompted such violence and what could have been done to prevent it abound. The widespread publicity generated by school shootings makes it seem that schools are now dangerous places and that the danger is increasing. But how common are school shootings? In fact, the number of homicides occurring in schools has actually declined in recent years. School-age children are at very low risk of becoming victims of homicide, and only 1 in 100 homicides of school-age children is associated with school. The vast majority occur elsewhere. Furthermore, children are hundreds of times more likely to be killed in accidents than by school violence. This is not to say that school administrators should not do what they can to prevent such tragedies in schools or on school grounds, but the risk of a child being killed in school is incredibly remote.

in 1999 and Virginia Tech University in 2007 have highlighted the problem of violence and have led to ongoing efforts to understand and curtail aggressive behavior. Unfortunately, the causes of violence are numerous and complex, making preventive intervention exceedingly challenging.

Even defining what constitutes aggression can be difficult. The intent and purpose of aggressive behaviors is to cause harm to others, but this broad definition quickly becomes imprecise. Few people would argue with the fact that physical assaults and murders involve aggressive acts, but what about other behaviors? Is it aggression when one child shoves another child on a playground? How about when one driver makes an obscene gesture toward another driver? What if a high school student spreads rumors about a classmate? Some people would consider each of these to be an act of aggression; others might disagree. At the very least, we need to recognize that aggression comes in many forms, and perceptions of whether or not something is aggressive are subjective.

Roots and Patterns of Human Aggression

Just as genetics may help to explain some prosocial behaviors, our evolutionary history also offers insight into our aggressive tendencies. Animals show aggression toward other members of their species to gain territory and mate preference, primarily to increase the likelihood of survival and reproduction. At least some aggressive behavior among humans may be attributable to similar historical tendencies, which life in modern societies has altered. Some evidence for this can be found in gender differences in aggression (discussed below). It is also clear that the hormone testosterone is linked with aggressive behavior. As levels of testosterone rise, so does the tendency to engage in aggressive behavior. It is important to note that much of the research on testosterone is correlational in nature—meaning that it establishes a statistical association without necessarily demonstrating that testosterone causes aggression. Such a link would also arise if a release of testosterone occurred as a consequence of aggressive behavior rather than as a cause. Still, a large body of animal research reveals some effects of insufficient or excessive testosterone. Powerful animals such as bulls cease nearly all aggression when deprived of testosterone through castration, and young female monkeys exhibit increased aggressive behavior after being exposed to elevated testosterone levels prior to birth. Much research remains to be done but biology and evolutionary roots clearly play a role in aggressive behavior.

But human aggression is obviously affected by more than biology and evolutionary forces. Learning plays a powerful role as well. In a now famous experiment, psychologist Albert Bandura and his colleagues had some children watch an adult aggressively hit and kick an inflatable doll. Other children watched a calm adult who did not behave aggressively toward the doll. When the children were later placed in a situation where they experienced frustration and were in

Longitudinal research showed that people exposed to violent television as young children exhibited more aggressive behavior years later as adults. *(Aaron Escobar. Wikipedia)*

the presence of the inflatable doll, those who had observed the aggressive adult behaved far more aggressively toward the doll than those who had watched the calm adult. This was the beginning of a long history of research demonstrating that children learn aggression from others. It is worth noting that the aggressive behavior occurs whether those modeling aggression are viewed in person or on television. Another interesting finding was that models of aggression need not be human—even violent cartoons have the potential to increase aggressive behavior in children.

There is also a body of research demonstrating a link between being the target of aggressive behavior and later demonstrating similar behavior. One interesting and controversial area of research concerns corporal punishment of children. Research shows rather clearly that children who are subjected to corporal punishment such as spanking are more likely to exhibit aggressive behavior both during childhood and as adults than are children who are not spanked. Like the findings concerning testosterone, however, these studies demonstrate a link without showing with certainty that spanking is the cause of children's aggression. After all, the same link would appear if children who behaved aggressively were the ones most likely to be spanked. Nonetheless, long term studies do suggest that subjecting children to corporal punishment may in fact cause later aggressive behavior.

In endeavoring to understand the causes of human aggression, researchers have observed many interesting patterns of aggressive tendencies. Perhaps one of the most interesting is the pattern of gender differences. Ask yourself the following question: Who are more aggressive, men or women? If you are like many people, your immediate response will be that men are more aggressive. If so you are partially correct, particularly with respect to physical forms of aggression. In nearly all parts of the world, men commit the vast majority of murders and other violent crimes and are generally more likely to get into physical fights when arguments arise. This sex differential in aggressive behavior begins very early in life. Even young boys are more physically aggressive than young girls. Several factors likely contribute to this differential. First, boys and men have greater levels of testosterone in their bodies, and (as noted above) greater testosterone levels are associated with greater aggression. In addition, boys and girls tend to experience very different socialization processes. Boys who behave aggressively tend to receive more social rewards for such behavior. This is not to say that adults consciously reinforce aggressive behavior in boys; what it means in a general sense is that boys often experience rewards such as popularity and social dominance when they behave aggressively, whereas girls more frequently face potential punishments for exhibiting similar behavior.

Whereas most research on aggressive behavior has centered on physical aggression, contemporary researchers have explored a wider variety of harmful interpersonal behavior. Researchers John Archer and Sarah Coyne, after an extensive review of past research, concluded that girls may not be less aggressive than boys but rather tend to engage in nonphysical aggression. For example, girls seem more likely to engage in **relational aggression** that is characterized by behaviors such as spreading rumors, ignoring, ostracizing, or embarrassing others, and violating others' trust. In additional work on the topic, Archer found that in some cases women may even match men in physical aggression. He cited evidence that in intimate relationships, women are equally or more likely to be physically abusive towards men as the reverse. The difference, according to Archer, is that men tend to inflict greater damage due to their greater strength. Interestingly, research indicates that the gender difference in physical aggression exists even when the underlying emotions experienced by men and women are the same. That is, men and women may experience the same anger but do not respond to it in the same way. In any case, the one thing that is clear about gender differences in aggression is that they are unclear.

Gender differences in aggression seem to apply across many cultures, but there are also interesting differences among various subcultures within larger cultures. In the United States, for example, people living in the South experience more violence than those living in the North, and African Americans experience more violence than members of other ethnic groups. The reasons for these differences are difficult to isolate but in many cases they may be due to socialization that validates (or least condones) aggressive behavior, the influence of poverty, and the importance that many individuals feel to physically defend themselves when their personal or family honor has been threatened.

Situational Influences

You may not be surprised to learn that people are more likely to become aggressive when they are frustrated. That is, when something or someone is blocking their pursuit of some objective, the emotions that result can trigger aggression. For example, imagine you are driving to work and there is someone in front of you who is driving well below the speed limit. Assuming you are unable to pass this driver's car, you may find that your sense of frustration and even anger increases rather quickly because your progress is being impeded. This is often cited as the primary cause of road rage. When people feel frustrated, they sometimes lash out at others. Frustrated people certainly do not always behave aggressively, but they are more likely to do so than people who are not frustrated.

The presence of **aggressive cues** in our environment also increases the likelihood of aggression. Items such as guns or other weapons, for example, are associated with aggression. Research has in fact shown that aggressive thoughts are activated in people who view photographs of guns. In one very interesting study, participants who were provoked by a partner in the study delivered (supposed) electric shocks to the person responsible for the provocation. When a gun was used as a study prop, the participants delivered more shocks to the perpetrator than when the researchers used badminton rackets as a prop. Clearly, the presence of an aggressive cue—even one unrelated to one's immediate activity—can increase aggressive behavior.

People are also more likely to behave aggressively when they are in a bad mood. This is why events that trigger negative moods often precipitate violence. You may have observed people behaving aggressively after a local sports team lost a game. People who feel strongly about a favorite team may become aggressive, especially toward members (or fans) of the winning team. Interestingly, the violence can even occur before the game begins. When rival teams or their fans come into contact, the perceived threat that the opposing side represents can create the mood necessary for violence to occur. Even things such as unpleasant odors and high temperatures can affect mood strongly enough to increase aggressive behavior.

Consumption of alcohol also tends to increase aggressive behavior. This effect occurs at least in part because alcohol lowers our usual inhibitions against acting aggressively. Imagine again the fans of two rival teams at a sporting event. The negative mood created by a potential loss and the presence of the opposition can lead to violence. Alcohol consumption, which is quite common at such events, acts as a catalyst to increase the risk of aggression. In general, alcohol probably plays a role in nearly half of all violent crimes. Alcohol may also play a role through its capacity to make us feel aroused. Research shows that people experiencing physiological arousal are more likely to behave aggressively. In one study, simply pedaling an exercise bike caused participants to act more aggressively than people not engaged in this activity. This effect emerged in the absence of any other emotional triggers or aggressive cues.

Any discussion of the role of situational factors in aggression must include some mention of media effects. People concerned about this issue have targeted many forms of contemporary media such as movies, television, music, and video games, and the research indicates that their concerns are well founded. It is well established that people who watch others behaving aggressively are more likely to exhibit aggressive behaviors themselves. This is an important consideration given the sheer volume of television viewing. Estimates vary, but Americans watch approximately 7 hours of television per day and many of the programs being watched contain violent content. Additional research suggests that exposure to violent video games or music lyrics is linked with increased acceptance of and greater tendency to participate in violence. Perhaps most important is the aforementioned longitudinal research demonstrating that people exposed to violent television as young children exhibited more aggressive behavior years later as adults. Two researchers, Brad Bushman and Rowell Huesmann, concluded, "the correlation between media violence and aggression is only slightly smaller than that between smoking and lung cancer."

REDUCING AGGRESSION

As noted earlier in this chapter, the causes of aggression are complex and any single aggressive behavior is caused by a variety of short- and long-term factors. However, there are steps that may help to reduce violence and aggression overall, and the strategies most likely to be successful are those that target situational influences. Reducing aggression means reducing the most controllable causes of aggression. We have seen that the presence of weapons tends to increase aggressive behaviors, so one strategy is to make weapons less prevalent. The ongoing social and political debates about gun ownership show that this is a rather difficult proposition to enact, but most researchers studying aggression related cues would argue that this would likely have a positive effect. Given that people—especially children—learn aggressive behavior from influential models, it is important that adults model appropriate restraint when dealing with difficult situations. Reducing negative mood and teaching adaptive strategies for dealing with frustration might also prove beneficial. It is also critical to find ways to reward children for behaviors that are helpful rather than harmful. Media influences can be particularly difficult to change because media decision making is generally based on profit rather than social responsibility. However, public dismay at excessive media violence has the potential to reduce the prevalence of aggressive programming. Needless to say, aggression is firmly woven throughout human societies and will never disappear. We can, however, take small steps to reduce its prevalence and ameliorate its influence.

SUMMARY

In this chapter we have explored some of the factors that make people likely to help or hurt each other. People often go to great lengths to help others, even when there is little chance of receiving anything other than a good feeling in return for doing so. A variety of factors help to determine whether someone will help in a given situation, and it is still unclear to what extent prosocial behavior is rooted in our genetic makeup or is a consequence of learning. The same can be said of aggressive and antisocial behavior. Many factors make aggression more or less likely in general, but understanding individual acts of aggression is often very difficult. Social psychologists have identified ways to increase the likelihood of prosocial behavior and reduce the likelihood of antisocial behavior, but strategies that are easily implemented in controlled laboratory settings are often difficult to implement in the real world. Nevertheless, we now understand far more about these behaviors than we did in the past, and the search for effective ways to increase desirable behaviors continues.

Further Reading

Berkowitz, Leonard. *Aggression: Its Causes, Consequences, and Control.* New York, New York; England: McGraw-Hill Book Company, 1993.

Schroeder, David A., Louis A. Penner, John F. Dovidio, and Jane A. Piliavin. *The Psychology of Helping and Altruism: Problems and Puzzles*. New York: McGraw-Hill, 1995.

CHAPTER 7

AFTERWORD

This book has presented a wide variety of topics in the field of social psychology. Hopefully, it has conveyed to you a number of important concepts that will help you better understand the complexities of human behavior. You have learned that people's behavior while they are part of a group is often radically different from their behavior while alone. You have also come to understand that our views of the world are determined by many factors, some of which are largely beyond our conscious awareness, and that our overt behavior is sometimes inconsistent with our internal thoughts and feelings. You probably now have greater awareness of the factors that make us likely to help or hurt others, and you're aware that personality and moral values are but a small part of the picture. You have become more familiar with the importance of relationships to healthy human functioning, and you know that our relationships result from a host of complex factors as well as from by sheer chance. As is the case in so many areas of psychology, research in social psychology sometimes substantiates what we think we know about people, but it frequently reminds us that our intuition about what people do and why is often inaccurate or incomplete.

This brief book merely scratches the surface of the very broad discipline of social psychology. There are, of course, other areas of study that are also relevant to our understanding of how people's thoughts and behavior are affected by the behavior of others. One example is the field of person perception. Researchers in this field study how we come to form impressions of people, and how first impressions, stereotypes, and self-fulfilling prophecies affect interpersonal interaction. One of the key goals of impression formation research is understanding how we draw inferences about the causes of behavior. Social psychologists refer to our assumptions about people's behavior as attributions, because we tend to attribute most behaviors to some specific cause. We can attribute a person's behavior to internal forces (such as their intelligence or personality) or to constraints in the person's environment. Thus, a person who cuts you off in traffic may be foolish or rude, or he or she may be rushing to help a loved one who is in trouble. Interestingly, we tend to make internal attributions in such situations, meaning that we assume an internal cause rather than a situational one even though we have no objective information either way. Researchers have called this tendency the fundamental attribution error. Research on how we form impressions is also relevant to understanding our own behavior. Anyone who has ever had a job interview or asked someone on a date knows that we often make active efforts to control how other people form impressions of us.

In addition to the fact that the details and nuance of social psychological research go far beyond what can be covered in this book, it is also the case that some of the specific conclusions described in this book would vary based on the characteristics of the people included in any given study. It is important to recognize that the vast majority of research in psychology has been conducted by researchers in the United States and other Western countries. This certainly does not discredit their findings, but we must consider how broadly those findings can be generalized on a global level. Do the relationship development patterns that researchers have observed in the United States also occur in China? Do people in African nations respond to compliance pressures in the same way as people from, say northern European cultures? For that matter, do people in northern Africa respond in the same way as people in living in the southeastern part of the continent?

Cross-cultural research in psychology has been growing for several decades. One broad domain of comparison is that of individualistic versus collectivistic cultures. Individualistic cultures (such as those in the United States and Western Europe, for example) are cultures that emphasize individual achievement. In these cultures, people are rewarded in various ways for drawing attention to themselves and setting themselves apart from the crowd. In contrast, collectivistic cultures, prevalent in most regions of Asia, emphasize group cohesion and cooperation. In these cultures, an individual who attempts to emphasize personal achievement sometimes experiences negative consequences. A culture's orientation toward individualism or collectivism is ingrained in its members from a very early age and affects all kinds of attitudes and behavior. As just one example, the fundamental attribution error that you read about above occurs much more strongly in individualistic rather than in collectivistic cultures. That is, the tendency to attribute people's behavior to internal forces is more likely in cultures where individualism is paramount. In cultures that emphasize social harmony and promotion of group well-being, there is more of a tendency to recognize the potential influence of situational factors on an individual's behavior.

The reference section of this book provides a lengthy list of additional sources that you can explore to further develop your understanding of social psychology. The books and articles are but a few of the thousands of publications you might seek out depending on what topics interest you the most. As you study psychological theory and research, you will notice more and more examples of psychology at work in your everyday life. Researchers have been studying social psychology for more than a century. They have given us amazing insights into human behavior, and the research continues to yield fascinating new information each year. Perhaps the most interesting reality of all is that when it comes to understanding people, we will never run out of questions.

GLOSSARY

aggressive cues Objects, such as guns or knives, that are associated with aggression.

antisocial behaviors Behaviors that are intended to hurt other people.

attachment Relationship styles between children and their caregivers that can be associated with subsequent relationship patterns as adults.

attitude A tendency to respond in a particular way to particular people, groups, objects, or situations.

availability heuristic The tendency to base our decisions and beliefs on images that most readily come to mind.

brainstorming A strategy intended to help groups produce as many novel ideas as possible.

bystander effect The reduced likelihood of helping when one is in a group.

classical conditioning Learning associations between previously unrelated stimuli.

cognitive dissonance Mental tension that occurs when a person simultaneously holds conflicting thoughts.

cohesiveness The degree to which the members of a group feel close ties and commitment to the group's identity.

compliance Behavior change that occurs in response to specific pressure from someone who has no genuine authority.

confirmation bias The tendency to notice and remember information that confirms one's expectations.

conformity The tendency to act in ways that are consistent with the behavior of others.

deindividuation The loss of individual identity in favor of group identity.

discrimination Biased behavior toward people, generally prompted by their membership in some group.

door-in-the-face technique A compliance technique that involves making an excessive request that is likely to be rejected, followed by a smaller request.

elaboration likelihood model A model proposing that persuasion can take place along multiple cognitive routes.

foot-in-the-door technique A compliance technique that involves making a small request that is likely to be accommodated, followed by a greater or more extensive request.

group A gathering of people whose interests are interdependent.

group polarization The tendency for a group's views to become more polarized than individual members' views.

groupthink An effect that occurs in highly cohesive groups in which dissenting views are suppressed.

halo effect The tendency to identify one positive trait in a person and then assume that person has many other positive traits.

illusory correlation An exaggerated sense of the association between two variables or characteristics.

implicit attitude An attitude that is out of a person's conscious awareness.

ingroup The group of people with whom a person identifies.

jigsaw classroom A strategy for reducing prejudice and discrimination; involves cooperative learning and superordinate goals.

kinship selection The tendency for people to help close genetic relatives more readily than they would help more distantly related people.

low-ball technique A compliance technique that occurs when one party changes the terms of an agreement after the agreement has been reached.

matching hypothesis A theory that presumes people will enter into relationships with others who are similar in attractiveness to themselves.

mere-exposure effect The tendency for someone to increasingly like a stimulus after repeated encounters with that stimulus.

minimal group paradigm A research technique in which trivial differences between groups are emphasized and made meaningful.

norm of reciprocity The social norm to respond in kind when someone has given you something.

norms   Guidelines in a group's culture that steer members' behavior.

obedience   Following orders from someone in authority.

observational learning   Learning from watching and imitating other people.

operant conditioning   A type of learning where behavior is controlled by its consequences.

outgroup   People whose group identity is different from one's own.

outgroup homogeneity effect   The tendency to perceive members of one's outgroup as more much more similar to each other than to members of one's ingroup.

persuasion   Occurs when a person's attitude about something changes because of the influence of someone else.

prejudice   Negative emotions toward people prompted by their membership in some group.

prosocial behaviors   Behaviors that are intended to help other people.

racism   Biased emotions and treatment of others that is prompted by their race.

relational aggression   Behaviors such as spreading rumors, ignoring, ostracizing, or embarrassing others, and violating others' trust.

relationship   A social connection between two or more people.

risky shift   A tendency for groups to make more risky decisions than individuals.

schema   A mental set of expectations that help to organize information about the world.

self-fulfilling prophecy   A process where a person has no choice but to act in way that confirms another person's expectations.

self-perception theory   A theory that people develop their attitudes by observing their own behavior.

sexism   Biased emotions and treatment of others prompted by their gender.

sexual orientation   One's tendency to experience sexual interest in people of the opposite sex (heterosexual orientation), same sex (homosexual orientation), or both sexes (bisexual orientation).

social dilemma   A situation where one must decide whether to sacrifice some aspect of one's individual interests for the greater good.

social facilitation   An improvement in performance that occurs when observers are present.

social inhibition   A reduction in performance that one experiences when performing a complex task in front of observers.

social loafing   The effect that people often do not work as hard when they are members of a group than they do when working individually.

stereotypes   Beliefs about people who are members of certain groups.

stereotype threat   Fear that emerges when one is confronted with a situation that may confirm a negative stereotype about one's own group.

subliminal   Stimuli outside of one's conscious awareness.

superordinate goals   Objectives that require group cooperation for successful completion.

triangular theory of love   A theory that there are many types of love consisting of various combinations of three basic components: intimacy, passion, and commitment.

BIBLIOGRAPHY

Ajzen, Icek, and Martin Fishbein. The Influence of Attitudes on Behavior. In *The Handbook of Attitudes*, eds. Dolores Albarracín, Blair T. Johnson and Mark P. Zanna, 173–221. Mahwah, N.J.: Lawrence Erlbaum Associates Publishers, 2005.

Allport, Gordon W. *The Nature of Prejudice*. Oxford, England: Addison-Wesley, 1954.

Archer, John. "Sex Differences in Aggression Between Heterosexual Partners: A Meta-analytic Review." *Psychological Bulletin* 126, no. 5 (Sep 2000): 651–680.

Archer, John, and Sarah M. Coyne. "An Integrated Review of Indirect, Relational, and Social Aggression." *Personality and Social Psychology Review* 9, no. 3 (2005): 212–230.

Arkes, Hal R. Some Practical Judgment and Decision-making Research. In *Individual and Group Decision Making: Current Issues*. Ed. N. John Castellan Jr. 3–18. Hillsdale, N.J.; UK: Lawrence Erlbaum Associates, 1993.

Asch, S.E. *Effects of Group Pressure Upon the Modification and Distortion of Judgments*. Oxford, England: Carnegie Press, 1951.

Bandura, A., Dorothea Ross, and Sheila A. Ross. "Transmission of Aggression Through Imitation of Aggressive Models." *The Journal of Abnormal and Social Psychology* 63, no. 3 (Nov 1961): 575–582.

Batson, Charles Daniel. *The Altruism Question: Toward a Social-psychological Answer*. Hillsdale, N.J.; UK: Lawrence Erlbaum Associates, 1991.

Bem, Daryl J. "Self-perception: An Alternative Interpretation of Cognitive Dissonance Phenomena. *Psychological Review* 74, no. 3 (May 1967): 183–200.

Berkowitz, Alan D. An Overview of the Social Norms Approach. *In Changing the Culture of College Drinking: A Socially Situated Prevention Campaign*, eds. Linda C. Lederman, and Lea P. Stewart, 193–214. Creskill: Hampton Press, 2005.

Berkowitz, Leonard. *Aggression: Its Causes, Consequences, and Control*. New York; UK: Mcgraw-Hill Book Company, 1993.

Berkowitz, Leonard, and Anthony Lepage. "Weapons as Aggression-eliciting Stimuli." *Journal of Personality and Social Psychology* 7, no. 2 (Oct 1967): 202–207.

Bohner, Gerd, and Norbert Schwarz. Attitudes, Persuasion, & Behavior. In *Blackwell Handbook of Social Psychology: Intraindividual Processes*, eds. Abraham Tesser and Norbert Schwarz, 413–435. Malden, Mass.: Wiley-Blackwell, 2003.

Bornstein, Robert F. "Exposure and Affect: Overview and Meta-analysis of Research, 1968–1987." *Psychological Bulletin* 106, no. 2 (1989): 265–289.

Brehm, Sharon S., Saul M. Kassin, and Steven Fein. *Social Psychology*. 6th ed. Boston, Mass: Houghton Mifflin, 2005.

Bushman, Brad J., and L. Rowell Huesmann. Effects of Televised Violence on Aggression. In *Handbook of Children and the Media*, eds. Dorothy G. Singer and Jerome L. Singer, 223–254. Thousand Oaks, Calif.: Sage, 2001.

Byrne, D. "Interpersonal Attraction and Attitude Similarity." *The Journal of Abnormal and Social Psychology* 62, no. 3 (1961): 713–715.

Centers for Disease Control and Prevention. "School-Assisted Homicides—United States, 1992-2006." Available at http://www.cdc.gov/mmwr/preview/mmwrhtml/mm5702a1.htm. Accessed July 24, 2010.

Chaiken, Shelly. "Communicator Physical Attractiveness and Persuasion." *Journal of Personality and Social Psychology* 37, no. 8 (Aug 1979): 1387–1397.

Cialdini, Robert B. *Influence: Science and Practice*. 4th ed. Boston, Mass.: Allyn and Bacon, 2001.

Cialdini, Robert B., John T. Cacioppo, Rodney Bassett, and John A. Miller. "Low-ball Procedure for Producing Compliance: Commitment Then Cost. *Journal of Personality and Social Psychology* 36, no. 5 (May 1978): 463–476.

Cialdini, Robert B., Joyce E. Vincent, Stephen K. Lewis, Jose Catalan, Diane Wheeler, and Betty Lee Darby. "Reciprocal Concessions Procedure for Inducing Compliance: The Door-in-the-face Technique." *Journal of Personality and Social Psychology* 31, no. 2 (Feb 1975): 206–215.

Danaher, Kelly, and Christian S. Crandall. "Stereotype Threat in Applied Settings Reexamined." *Journal of Applied Social Psychology* 38, no. 6 (Jun 2008): 1639–1655.

Darley, John M., and Bibb Latane. "Bystander Intervention in Emergencies: Diffusion of Responsibility." *Journal of Personality and Social Psychology* 8, no. 4, part 1 (Apr 1968): 377–383.

Darley, John M., and C. Daniel Batson. "From Jerusalem to Jericho: A Study of Situational and Dispositional Variables in Helping Behavior." *Journal of Personality and Social Psychology* 27, no. 1 (Jul 1973): 100–108.

Dawkins, Richard. *The Selfish Gene.* Oxford: Oxford University Press, 1989.

Eastwick, Paul W., Eli J. Finkel, Daniel Mochon, and Dan Ariely. "Selective versus Unselective Romantic Desire: Not All Reciprocity Is Created Equal." *Psychological Science* 18, no. 4 (2007): 317–319.

Efran, Michael G., and E. W.J. Patterson. "Voters Vote Beautiful: The Effect of Physical Appearance on a National Election." *Canadian Journal of Behavioural Science/Revue canadienne des sciences du comportement* 6, no. 4 (1974): 352–356.

Federal Bureau of Investigation. "Uniform Crime Reports." http://www.fbi.gov/ucr/ucr.htm. Accessed July 24, 2010.

Festinger, Leon. *A Theory of Cognitive Dissonance.* Stanford University Press, 1962.

Festinger, Leon, and James M. Carlsmith. "Cognitive Consequences of Forced Compliance." *The Journal of Abnormal and Social Psychology* 58, no. 2 (Mar 1959): 203–210.

Festinger, Leon, Stanley Schachter, and Kurt Back. *Social Pressures in Informal Groups: A Study of Human Factors in Housing.* Oxford: Harper, 1950.

Freedman, Jonathan L., and Scott C. Fraser. "Compliance Without Pressure: The Foot-in-the-door Technique." *Journal of Personality and Social Psychology* 4, no. 2 (Aug 1966): 195–202.

Gailliot, Matthew T., B. Michelle Peruche, E. Ashby Plant, and Roy F. Baumeister. "Stereotypes and Prejudice in the Blood: Sucrose Drinks Reduce Prejudice and Stereotyping." *Journal of Experimental Social Psychology* 45, no. 1 (Jan 2009): 288–290.

Gottman, John M., and Nan Silver. *Why Marriages Succeed or Fail and How You Can Make Yours Last.* New York: Fireside Books, 1994.

Hazan, Cindy, and Phillip Shaver. "Romantic Love Conceptualized as an Attachment Process." *Journal of Personality and Social Psychology* 52, no. 3 (1987): 511–524.

Hoss, Rebecca A., and Judith H. Langlois. Infants Prefer Attractive Faces. In *The Development of Face Processing in Infancy and Early Childhood: Current Perspectives*, 27–38. Hauppauge, N.Y.: Nova Science Publishers, 2003.

Janis, Irving L. *Victims of Groupthink: A Psychological Study of Foreign-policy Decisions and Fiascoes*. Oxford: Houghton Mifflin, 1972.

King, Michael, Joanna Semlyen, Sharon See Tai, Helen Killaspy, David Osborn, Dmitri Popelyuk, and Irwin Nazareth. "A Systematic Review of Mental Disorder, Suicide, and Deliberate Self-harm in Lesbian, Gay, and Bisexual People." *BMC Psychiatry* 8 (2008).

Latane, Bibb, and John M. Darley. *The Unresponsive Bystander: Why Doesn't He Help?* New York: Meredith, 1970.

Lewin, Kurt. *Resolving Social Conflicts: Selected Papers on Group Dynamics*. Oxford, UK: Harper, 1948.

Milgram, Stanley. Behavioral Study of Obedience. *The Journal of Abnormal and Social Psychology* 67, no. 4 (Oct 1963): 371–378.

Moreland, Richard L., and Scott R. Beach. 1992. "Exposure Effects in the Classroom: The Development of Affinity Among Students." *Journal of Experimental Social Psychology* 28, no. 3 (1992): 255–276.

Nelson, Todd D. (Ed). *Handbook of Prejudice, Stereotyping, and Discrimination*. New York, N:Y: Psychology Press, 2009.

Osborn, Alex F. *Applied Imagination: Principles and Procedures of Creative Problem-solving*. New York: Scribner, 1957.

Parks, Craig D., and Lawrence J. Sanna. *Group Performance and Interaction*. Boulder, Colo.: Westview Press, 1999.

Perdue, Charles W., John F. Dovidio, Michael B. Gurtman, and Richard B. Tyler. "Us and Them: Social Categorization and the Process of Intergroup Bias." *Journal of Personality and Social Psychology* 59, no. 3 (Sep 1990): 475-486.

Perloff, Richard M. *The Dynamics of Persuasion: Communication and Attitudes in the 21st Century*. 3rd ed.. New York: Taylor & Francis Group/Lawrence Erlbaum Associates, 2008.

Petty, Richard E., and John T. Cacioppo. *Communication and Persuasion: Central and Peripheral Routes to Attitude Change*. New York: Springer-Verlag, 1986.

Reis, Harry T., and Susan Sprecher, Eds. *Encyclopedia of Human Relationships* (Vols. 1–3). Thousand Oaks, Calif.: Sage Publications, 2009.

Roisman, Glenn I., Eric Clausell, Ashley Holland, Keren Fortuna, and Chryle Elieff. "Adult Romantic Relationships as Contexts of Human Development: A Multimethod Comparison of Same-sex Couples with Opposite-sex Dating, Engaged, and Married Dyads." *Developmental Psychology* 44, no. 1 (2008): 91–101.

Schroeder, David A., Louis A. Penner, John F. Dovidio, and Jane A. Piliavin. *The Psychology of Helping and Altruism: Problems and Puzzles.* New York: McGraw-Hill, 1995.

Sherif, Muzafer, O.J. Harvey, B. Jack White, William R. Hood, and Carolyn W. Sherif. *The Robbers Cave Experiment.* Middletown, Conn.: Wesleyan University Press, 1988.

Silvia, Paul J. "Deflecting Reactance: The Role of Similarity in Increasing Compliance and Reducing Resistance." *Basic and Applied Social Psychology* 27, no. 3 (Sept 2005): 277–284.

Slater, Alan, Charlotte Von der Schulenburg, Elizaabeth Brown, Marion Badenoch, George Butterworth, Sonia Parsons, and Curtis Samuels. "Newborn Infants Prefer Attractive Faces." Infant Behavior & Development 21, no. 2 (1998): 345–354.

Stangor, Charles (Ed.) *Stereotypes and Prejudice: Essential Readings. Key Readings in Social Psychology.* New York: Psychology Press, 2000.

Steele, Claude M. "A Threat in the Air: How Stereotypes Shape Intellectual Identity and Performance." *American Psychologist* 52, no. 6 (Jun 1997): 613–629.

Sternberg, Robert J. "A Triangular Theory of Love." *Psychological Review* 93, no. 2 (1986): 119–135.

Sussman, Norman. "In Session with Dennis S. Charney, MD: Resilience to Stress." *Primary Psychiatry* 13, no. 8 (2006): 39–41.

Triplett, Norman. "The Dynamogenic Factors in Pacemaking and Competition." *The American Journal of Psychology* 9, no. 4, (Jul 1898): 507–533.

Tuckman, Bruce W. "Developmental Sequence in Small Groups." *Psychological Bulletin* 63, no. 6 (Jun 1965): 384–399.

Twenge, Jean M., and W. Keith Campbell. *The Narcissism Epidemic: Living in the Age of Enlightenment.* New York: Free Press, 2009.

INDEX

Note: Page numbers followed by *g* indicate glossary entries.